D0933813

Vigil in Benicarló

Vigil in Benicarló

Manuel Azaña

Translated with an Introduction
by Josephine Stewart and Paul Stewart

Rutherford ● Madison ● Teaneck
Fairleigh Dickinson University Press
London and Toronto: Associated University Presses

Associated University Presses, Inc.
4 Cornwall Drive
East Brunswick, N.J. 08816

R0147387728
HUM

Associated University Presses Ltd
69 Fleet Street
London EC4Y 1EU, England

Associated Univerity Presses
Toronto M5E 1A7, Canada

Library of Congress Cataloging in Publication Data

Azaña, Manuel, 1880–1940.
 Vigil in Benicarló.

 Translation of: La velada en Benicarló.
 1. Spain—History—Civil War, 1936–1939—Drama.
I. Title.
PQ6601.Z3V413   1982   862'.62   81-65339
ISBN 0-8386-3093-6   AACR2

Printed in the United States of America

Contents

Translator's Introduction

More succinctly and dramatically than any other literary work of the period, Manuel Azaña's *Vigil in Benicarló* presents in all of its complexity the terrible frustration felt by liberals in the mid-twentieth century. He does not tell a story; he puts forth Spain in the midst of her tragic civil war in terms of the actual life of these times, exploring various aspects of historical and philosophical reality. World interest focused on Spain at this time, and many foreign authors participated in the war and wrote about it—Orwell, Malraux, Koestler, and Hemingway among them. As the foremost Spanish statesman of the 1930s (he was president of the Republic when he wrote this dialogue) Azaña had a quite different perspective. He writes with the awareness of a political insider, the perception of a Spanish intellectual, and the sensitivity of an artist. A practiced literary man, dramatist, biographer, novelist, translator, and essayist, he used his talents to transcend the story of his own adventures and to depict the war as an integral part of the whole Spanish tradition, without ever losing contact with real life.

The book has its own history, dramatically suited to its content and context. Written in April 1937, fourteen months after the harrowing election that had restored Azaña to political power, nine months after the civil war's outbreak, it shows his frustrations in trying to head a nation at war. He dictated the final draft during riots, a civil-war-within-a-civil-war that rocked Barcelona in the period from 3 May to 8

May. He and his household found themselves under siege in the Catalan parliament building, their lives endangered. Dictating it, he saw this work as his possible valedictory message. Garcés, "former minister" and Azaña's most obvious mouthpiece in the dialogue, explains his conduct and attitude in a way that clearly reflects the author's own position.

Too controversial to publish during the war, his manuscript crossed into France with its author's baggage on 5 February 1939, four days ahead of Franco's army. Cipriano Rivas-Cherif, Azaña's friend and brother-in-law, pictures the former president later that year, reading parts of his unpublished *Vigil* to the exiled family. With Jean Camp, the two friends made a French translation; it appeared in Paris on 3 September, the day when France declared war on Germany. Inevitably the book failed to attract the attention its author anticipated, but even in that time of crisis it sold out an edition of 20,000 copies in less than a year. This French edition has special interest as having Azaña's personal imprimatur, the only edition that the author himself worked over. His numerous notations in his own copy of the first edition in its original language, published in Buenos Aires that same year, have provided the basis for subsequent Spanish editions. The book has also appeared in Italian.

Even some of Azaña's partisans protested that he had brought out the dialogue too soon. Its publication in Spain in 1974, toward the end of Franco's regime, symbolized the beginning of a new era in that country. References to forces headed by General Franco as "the rebels" and bitter attacks on fellow republicans began to seem part of the historical past. Yet the passage of time has increased the book's interest both as a document, a capsulation of a highly significant moment, and as a judgment. Azaña and his republic found themselves in a historical whirlwind that soon caught up the rest of the world; his dialogue represents a desperate effort to understand the long-range meaning of terrible current events. He showed acuity as a short-range prophet. By the time of his book's publication, just as he had predicted, Britain and

[8]

France faced the same German-Italian power that had defeated Spain's republic. His forecast about the price Nationalist Spain, Franco's Spain, would have to pay for Axis aid did not hit so close to the mark. Though the nation did not get off free, she played a somewhat independent role in World War II. Longer-range prophecies point to key questions not only about Spain's future but about the future of the world, because just as Spain's civil war blended into the Second World War, so her problems at this time mirrored those of all mankind in the twentieth century.

The dialogue flows from a confluence of intellectual and political talents rare, if not unique, in the twentieth century. Azaña was born in 1880 in Alcalá de Henares, near Madrid, where his family had played a part in local government for three generations. Experience as a student in the Augustinian school at the Escorial provided substance for his first book, and best-known novel, *Garden of the Monks* (serialized in his magazine *La Pluma,* 1921–22, published separately, 1927). He reached manhood just when literary and historical fashion, long discontented and dissident, was reacting to Spain's defeat by the United States in 1898 by rethinking the nation's meaning and mission.

Spain had stood as a major world power for four centuries from the glorious age of Ferdinand and Isabella. The year 1492, which ended an 800-year war between Christians and Moslems in the Iberian Peninsula, also spectacularly began an age when Spain's heraldic gyrfalcons ruled over one of the first world empires. Some consequent policies such as the expulsion of nonconforming elements of her population still provided material for discussion in Benicarló in 1937. However, the principal heritage for Azaña's generation was a sense of disorientation that followed the collapse of this world empire. The system or set of circumstances on which Spain's world power rested broke down late in the eighteenth century. By 1825 most of her American empire had dissolved into independent nations without her army and navy being able to do much about it. The nineteenth century brought great disruption at home, with a new order struggling to get

[9]

born while many elements of Spanish society, like the Carlists, clung determinedly to institutions that had represented the Golden Age's greatness. In this situation the army became political arbiter. Forty-three army pronunciamentos took place between 1814 and 1923. In the same period there arose the kind of militant leftist opposition that proved so frustrating in the 1930s.

Spain's defeat in 1898 and the consequent loss of much of her remaining empire brought a tremendous sense of loss, but it also inspired a generation of Spanish intellectuals to extraordinary achievement in redefining their nation's meaning. If the ghost of a lost empire still haunts the vigil in Benicarló, we also note concepts of enduring national greatness based on cultural achievement. Manuel Azaña lived out his life in the shadow of the illustrious Generation of '98. A second-magnitude literary figure as compared to its greatest stars, he belonged to the so-called Generation of 1914, which went on to find its own voice in dealing with the problems of post-1898 Spain.

Monarchy endured, supported by the army and propertied classes. Symbolizing this system, caciques, political bosses whose appellation derived from American Indian chiefs, controlled rural Spain. Growing anarchism, especially in industrial Barcelona and the rural South, suggested the system's weakness. Remnants of the empire seemed more important than ever; for one thing, they provided justification for the army budget. Yet continual wars for control in Morocco produced no decisive victories and caused popular disaffection. A 1909 demonstration in Barcelona against calling up reserves for Moroccan service became a general strike and popular insurrection. After a week it left more than a hundred people killed and one-third of the city's religious buildings damaged or destroyed. The Catholic Church, identified with traditional Spain and identifying with it, offered an obvious target for opponents of that tradition. Spain took no part in World War I, but depression, new troubles in Morocco, and fear caused by political disorder elsewhere in Europe all combined in 1923 to inspire the

[10]

postwar coup d'etat of General Miguel Primo de Rivera. Without deposing the king, and with an expressed intention to reorganize the state, Primo controlled the nation as dictator for six years.

This dictatorship caused Azaña to become seriously involved in politics with the formation of the Republican Action Party. Earlier signs of his dual vocation were his first published full-length book (1918), a study of the relationship of the army and government in France, and unsuccessful candidacies for the Cortes in 1918 and 1923. In 1926 his *Life of Don Juan Valera* won the National Prize for Literature. Valera, a man who considered diplomacy his vocation, was at the same time a major nineteenth-century novelist and literary figure. When Primo's dictatorship collapsed under the pressure of world depression and from lack of royal support, Azaña joined a coalition of republicans that made plans to step in and take charge of the state. This Coalition of San Sebastián went so far as to draw up a list of ministers for a future government. Identified with army reforms by his earlier book, Azaña got the ministry of war. This post became his in fact in April 1931 when the king lost control of the nation.

The Republic was proclaimed after municipal elections went strongly against royalist candidates. Uncertain about the army's position, King Alfonso XIII left Spain. The place of the army and of the Catholic Church in Spanish life stood as key problems for the new government, along with economic and social reform and the aspirations of Catalonia and the Basque provinces for autonomy. Controversies arising from republican responses to these problems provide the immediate background for the Benicarló dialogue. Initially the Church problem gave most trouble in the cities. On 11 May, less than a month after Alfonso's departure, mobs in Madrid vandalized a dozen churches, giving the signal for similar outrages elsewhere. Official government policy was even more serious. The new republican constitution took a strong position in regard to the Church. It did not stop at separation of church and state, which meant the end of a tax-supported clergy, but also made a frontal attack on the work of religious orders. The latter lost all property not directly required by their normal functions, with "normal functions" severely restricted, particularly in the area of nonconfessional teaching. Debates on these provisions surveyed the whole history of the Church's role in Spanish society. Azaña took an important part in these debates and emerged from them natural leader of the secular Republic. He became prime minister on 16 October 1931.

During the next two years the Republic achieved many of its goals; however, much remained unfinished, and inevitably opposition arose. Azaña held together an otherwise disparate coalition by emphasizing religious issues, but his opponents of the Right also found a common ground in these issues. At least in the short run, Azaña had great success with the army. Offering retirement at full pay to all officers willing to resign within thirty days' time, he greatly reduced the swollen officer corps and, presumably, eliminated many politician-officers. It was hoped that only dedicated, able officers would remain, but such men tended to resist civilian control and further reforms. In August 1932 General José Sanjurjo, originally at least neutral toward the Republic, revolted against it with the excuse that anarchy threatened. However, his move did not attract much support even from the military.

Sanjurjo's particular quarrel with the Republic stemmed from his removal as head of the Civil Guard because of fierce repression of disorders in Barcelona, Santander in the North, and Estremadura. Early dissatisfaction with the Republic focused in these areas. In the atmosphere of unity that came in the wake of this revolt, Azaña achieved another of his triumphs with passage of the Statute of Catalonia, granting a limited degree of autonomy to that province. Against very strong pressure from Barcelona for something like a completely independent Catalonia in a federated Spain, he succeeded in gaining acceptance of a Catalan government, named after the medieval *Generalitat,* which remained integrally part of the larger Spanish state.

[12]

A combination of factors acted to make the Republic's action in the very difficult area of economic reform, particularly land reform, less positive, decisive, and successful. Azaña's government, after all, confronted the same world depression that had brought down the Primo de Rivera regime and undermined the monarchy. Furthermore, international business interests distrusted a republican regime that favored any economic disturbance in Spain. Marcelino Domingo, with impossibly broad responsibilities as minister of agriculture, commerce, and industry, owed his post to Azaña's friendship and to his membership in the Catalan Radical Socialist Party rather than to his expertise. Political philosophy and personal ambition came between the cabinet's two Socialists, Indalecio Prieto and Francisco Largo Caballero, head of the General Union of Workers (UGT). Finally, in many parts of Spain anarcho-syndicalists dominated workers' politics; to them a centralized republic seemed little better than monarchy. Consequently, strikes and violence from workers in Barcelona, miners in the North, and peasants in the South plagued the Republic's first two years. The radical Iberian Anarchist Federation (FAI) organized to fight any tendency shown by the anarchist workers' Anarchist National Confederation (CNT) to cooperate with the government.

In the hot summer of 1933 the coalition that supported Azaña broke up. Twenty-five months of hard work had exhausted members of the first republican Cortes. Azaña's basically conservative economic program disappointed many Socialists, and anarcho-syndicalists bitterly resented government use of troops to quell disturbances identified with them. Political ambitions of men who wanted to supplant the prime minister played their part. At the same time rightist forces mustered the support of persons who feared socialism and were concerned about the religious issue. The November 1933 election resulted in a clear victory for conservative parties. Spain entered what its opponents came to call "the Black Biennium," which saw the policies of the previous two years reversed by nonenforcement of laws or through deci-

[13]

sions made by courts and governing boards. Leftist forces reacted by becoming more radical, and 1934 became a year of revolutionary action and government overreaction.

The climax came in October in Asturias and Barcelona. In Asturias a combination of CNT, UGT, Communists, and Trotskyites moved together to establish a new order dominated by workers. They had considerable initial success, actually taking over the city of Oviedo. The conservative Madrid government called in Moorish troops and Spanish legionnaires from Morocco who put down the revolt at the cost of more than 1,000 lives, most of them revolutionaries. A revolt at the same time in Barcelona fizzled, largely because various worker groups could not cooperate, but the *Generalitat* remained clearly compromised. The Madrid government, badly shaken, declared martial law, imposing censorship, suspending civil rights, and calling up army reserves. The general public knew very little of what actually happened; indeed these events in Asturias remain disputed today. This crisis greatly increased the tensions that exploded into civil war two years later.

Azaña had gone to Barcelona for a funeral when the October revolt broke out there. Although he had remained under continuous surveillance-protection and manifestly had nothing to do with the *Generalitat* or rioting, the Madrid government ordered him held, incommunicado, on a ship in Barcelona harbor until December. Meanwhile his enemies proclaimed him and "his band" responsible for the risings in both Catalonia and Asturias, and, generally, for all disorder in Spain. Press censorship prevented any reply. This all-out attack greatly increased Azaña's popularity with the Left. Angel Ossorio y Gallardo defended him at his trial. Prominent in public affairs for thirty years, a practicing lawyer and professor at the University of Madrid, and a framer of the 1931 constitution, Ossorio commanded respect. Besides, no evidence existed against Azaña.

Both sides were more frightened now than ever. The Left feared a military coup that would establish in Spain something like Italy's Fascist regime or the Nazi regime just then

[14]

taking over Germany. The Right feared a radical revolution and a workers' state like that of Soviet Russia. Both sides saw October's crisis as a near miss. The government maintained martial law through 1935, renewing each month their right to impose censorship and close down headquarters of opposition groups. The Catalan *Generalitat* stayed suspended, and tens of thousands of persons continued prisoners on political grounds. Pressure mounted. Youthful supporters of Left and Right clashed in Madrid's streets, as young gentlemen and young workers disputed each other's right to control the nation. The para-Fascist Falange remains the most famous of several rightist groups. People were killed on both sides. As after the Sanjurjo coup, leftist parties drifted together, a drift greatly enhanced by the Comintern policy of the Popular Front. Communists now felt willing to join with liberal groups in support for bourgeois reform and resistance to the Right. Thus, with Azaña as its natural leader, a coalition formed of various republican parties. Now even anarchists and Basque nationalists, always disinclined to become officially part of a centralized government, adopted a benevolent attitude.

Consequently, when President Niceto Alcalá-Zamora decided late in 1935 to hold elections the next year, in hopes that a center position would emerge, Spain split into two nearly equal political camps. Azaña's Popular Front stood for a return to the program of the Republic's first two years, greater momentum in land reform, and release of the political prisoners. Factions of the Right agreed on holding the line against revolution. With the largest voter participation ever, 73 percent, the Popular Front won a narrow victory. They benefited from the majority bloc system, which based representation in the Cortes on provincial majorities rather than on popular vote, so that Azaña's coalition came out with even more complete control than it had in 1931. At once representatives of the Right approached Francisco Franco, chief of the General Staff and a hero of the Moroccan wars, proposing that he lead a revolt. He refused.

The next five months determined the army revolt of 17–20

July and explain much of its support. Socialist workers, anarchists, and peasants now refused to settle for any compromise solution to their demands. Newspapers published inflammatory accounts of continuous agitation throughout Spain. In April the Cortes deposed centrist President Alcalá-Zamora, who had served since 1931. Azaña took his place, leaving Santiago Casares Quiroga, an inferior and unwell man, as prime minister because the Socialists refused to provide a candidate. Madrid began June with a strike involving 40,000 construction workers and 30,000 electricians and elevator repairmen, a strike complicated by clashes between UGT and CNT and also by the now habitual street fighting. Striking workers lived by helping themselves in grocery stores and by refusing to pay in restaurants. In July the Republic's friends claimed that things were improving; the generals revolted with the excuse that Spain, out of control, was about to go Communist.

Army pronunciamentos had varied success, but everywhere they depended on surprise and ruthless elimination of all opposition: officers who remained loyal to the Republic, civilian officials, and republicans. They directed their first thrust at local Socialist headquarters. Often insurgent commanders ployed by pretending to defend the Republic or using the legal republican device of declaring a state of martial law. They caught the Madrid government completely off guard. At first it tried to negotiate with the insurgents. A serious charge later directed against the government was its failure to distribute arms to the people, who, when armed, did frequently resist the rebellion with success. Garcés in the dialogue indicates Azaña's rationale. After all, at that moment, elements of the urban civilian population seemed hardly less insurgent than the generals. Largo Caballero's Left Socialists had been calling for revolution. At any rate, by 21 July, the morning when the Insurgent Montaña Barracks surrendered to a Madrid mob, the conspirators had gained control of Spanish North Africa, the Canaries and Balearics, Galicia, important positions in Old Castile, Andalusia, and Navarre, where the rebellion found Miguel Rivera of *Vigil in*

[16]

Benicarló. The Republic retained about two-thirds of Spain, including most of its Mediterranean coast and the industrial centers of Madrid and Barcelona.

At the Mediterranean naval base of Cartagena, sailors rose against their officers, preventing them from going over to the Insurgents. They also established a patrol to prevent the ferrying of Moroccan troops across into Spain. Because the momentum of the Insurgents' cause in Spain depended on reinforcement by this army, it became immediately necessary for them to secure foreign naval and air support. Mussolini had already committed himself to military aid for an eventual pronunciamento; now Hitler agreed to risk a stake in this round of the game of international politics. On 28 June German and Italian planes began an airlift of troops from North Africa to Spain. Antiaircraft fire from Spanish ships brought retaliation from the planes, and within a week republican naval patrols ended.

Azaña and his colleagues recognized that they, too, would require foreign support. Léon Blum, prime minister of France, headed a Popular Front coalition similar to that which governed Spain, and at first he intended to give the Republic all possible aid. Yet on 8 August the French closed their Spanish frontier, blocking even shipments of arms for which the Republic could pay. Blum found himself hampered in three ways. Consultation with the British government on 22 July made clear both its determination to avoid intervention in the civil war and its unwillingness to bolster France if she should become embroiled with Hitler on Spain's account. Furthermore, important elements in France, even within Blum's Popular Front coalition, felt, like many Britons, that the generals' victory might best serve their interests. Foreign investors had always felt concern about the potentially radical economics of the Spanish Republic and even more concern about its seemingly endemic disorder. Also, France's allies Belgium and Poland worried lest her involvement in Spain would weaken her ability to support them against a possible German attack.

As an alternative Blum unilaterally proclaimed a policy of

[17]

nonintervention, hoping that all powers would adhere to it, and closed the Franco-Spanish border. Twenty-seven nations met in London on 9 September to discuss and implement this policy, but the Germans and Italians merely used it as a screen for their active involvement. The London Committee refused to receive the republican government's evidence of German and Italian intervention because it came from a belligerent. Its members also took umbrage when the Spanish government presented its case to the League of Nations instead of waiting for Committee action. Protest to the League turned out to be a token gesture, however, because it refused to add Spain's problems to an already crowded agenda.

Active Soviet intervention in Spain stirred the London Committee into a semblance of life, as did other developments of the autumn and winter of 1936–37. Madrid did not fall immediately to Franco's forces, as anticipated, but offered heroic resistance. Fierce fighting on her outskirts, in suburbs like Carabanchel, caught popular imagination around the world. The Catholic Basques, who had important business ties with London, remained staunchly republican. Finally, a tremendous increase of Italian troops in Spain virtually canceled a bilateral "Gentlemen's Agreement" between Britain and Italy to maintain the Mediterranean status quo. On 8 January 1937 the British proposed a patrol of Spain's coast to prevent foreign intervention. Its implementation began about the time when Azaña wrote his *Vigil*. However, given the Nonintervention Committee's previous record and the strong sympathy of Portugal's President Antonio Salazar for the Insurgents, any such patrol did not promise to be effective. The Portuguese government treated Nationalist agents in Lisbon as Spain's real ambassadors rather than Claudio Sánchez Albornoz, the republican ambassador.

The Russians reacted more broadly in favor of the Republic than any other big nation, excepting the Mexicans. Informed of her plight by a controlled, highly sympathetic press, the Russian people held mass meetings and popular demonstrations. When the French closed their border in August, Russians already had sent two million dollars to pay for food and medical supplies. When it became clear that nonintervention meant nothing to Germany and Italy, the Soviet Union began openly to send war matériel paid for with Spanish gold. The Republic's people and government, unable to buy arms from any other major source, enthusiastically demonstrated their gratitude. Almost inevitably Soviet agents came to exercise influence within the Republic; as the war went on the question of Communist control of Spain arose. Azaña touches this problem somewhat defensively in his dialogue, and historians continue to debate it.

Meanwhile the government had a tremendous task in defending itself against a well-organized army commanded by most of Spain's regular top officers. At the same time it had to build a new army on the basis of Loyalist officers and a general populace many of whom had never fired a rifle. Once ferried across into Spain, the tough, well-trained African army of Moors and Legionnaires had great success in driving northward. Their dramatic advance gave great prestige to their commander, General Franco. Two months after fighting broke out they stood before Madrid, ready to join forces with armies advancing from Navarre and the North. That city's equally dramatic defense set guidelines for the rest of the war. On 6 November the government moved to Valencia, leaving Madrid an embattled fortress. On that night and the next, some 1,000 political prisoners, removed from the Model Prison ostensibly for transport to Valencia, were shot—a horrifying example of the atrocities that occurred on both sides. On 8 November the first International Brigades arrived in Madrid. Volunteers from all over the world, trained under Communist officers, they came to aid in defending Spain's Republic.

Leaving Madrid in the fall of 1936, Azaña emphasized his frustrations as president of the Republic by settling in Barcelona rather than in Valencia. The *Generalitat* assigned him an official residence in the Catalan parliament building, but he had virtually no contact with officials of the Catalan government. This period of his residence in Barcelona, until May 1937, during which time he conceived and wrote *Vigil in Benicarló,* proved a particularly unhappy time for the author-president. The war's first six months had brought a dramatic deterioration of his health. Garcés and Morales, the characters in the book who speak most clearly for their author, both remember occasions in this period when they wanted to die. The May riots came as a climax, or rather a nadir; Azaña's dialogue reflects this mood even better than his memoirs of the period.

Vigil in Benicarló shows hopelessness and a sense of futility about the condition of republican Spain in wartime. Largo Caballero, leader of the militantly dissident Socialists just before the war, had become prime minister on 4 September 1936. He very soon realized that all groups must band together for a successful war effort. In a similar reversal, on 4 November four anarchists joined the government on the eve of its move to Valencia. Anarchists had already joined the *Generalitat* a month earlier. However, as Garcés observes, mere service by these party members in the cabinet did not really commit other party members to cooperation. Largo also soon recognized that trained military men made better soldiers than untrained, enthusiastic civilians. Nonetheless, Málaga's fall on 9 February 1937 remained a monument to his earlier naiveté. The fall of Málaga, a big city that had overcome the original army coup, provided Azaña with a classic case to use in describing a pattern of crisis that plagued republican efforts: clashes between anarchists and Socialists, the heroic incompetence of amateur soldiers, the mystical belief that revolution and the people must inevitably win, and, finally, a combination of weakness and blundering at the helm that aroused suspicion of treason.

Azaña sardonically describes Barcelona's reaction to the initial victory of her populace over the insurrection. For many people in Barcelona this triumph on 19–20 July seemed to mark the beginning of a long-awaited and total social and economic revolution. Yet the same scene that inspired George Orwell, an English volunteer soldier, looked like chaos to

Azaña. Exploding with egalitarian enthusiasm and Catalan nationalism, Barcelona took only limited interest in a civil war that was determining the Republic's life or death. The region's militarily most effective force were the "uncontrollables" of Durruti's column. Buenaventura Durruti, former terrorist, FAI leader, and successful leader of the Barcelona people against the July insurrection, now led a troop of men on the northern Aragonese frontier. Along the way he wrought destruction and revolutionary justice, rationalizing that the people could rebuild all that they had built in the past. Yet he achieved no more than stabilization of the frontier, and he soon died in defense of Madrid. In the dialogue Doctor Lluch and Major Blanchart present personal, somewhat jaundiced accounts of the Barcelona revolution from civilian and military viewpoints, while Pastrana and Barcala defend its underlying concepts.

From Barcelona Azaña frequently traveled down to Valencia for conferences in Benicarló Palace, seat of the republican government. He would have known well the route whose dramatic description opens his book. Its careful construction, symbolistic and impressionistic, shows considerable meditation. On occasion they scheduled conferences at an inn halfway between the two great cities, in the village of Benicarló. Thus fiction blends with historical reality. Azaña shows the state of eastern Spain nine months into the war. An army officer's description of Málaga on the eve of its fall and Paquita Vargas's complaints about egalitarianism in the Barcelona theater and about pampered Fascist refugees give us the real world more accurately than contemporary newspapers. On another level the *Vigil* makes a profound effort to present Azaña's wartime experiences as meaningful propaganda and, even more, as meaningful historical analysis, the last resort of secularist man.

In his preface, Azaña, of course, denies that he has patterned his characters on actual individuals. Also predictably, readers have tried ever since to identify them with men who took part in the actual Benicarló discussions. Certainly Azaña's characters speak his own ideas. Garcés presents

[21]

Azaña's thoughts more succinctly than we can find them elsewhere, both in his analysis of Spain's Republic and in explanations of his own actions. Garcés's defeatism and the whole tone of the dialogue demonstrate the author's problems as wartime leader. Azaña's identification with the writer, Morales, presents a more interesting problem. His own conscious dualism, as writer and statesman, seems clear, and he puts into Morales's mouth some of his own most cherished ideas—ideas that appeared in his earliest writings and that he repeated after this book. Yet the very name *Eliseo Morales* stands as a ubiquitous pun on the way this character thinks and talks, although Azaña's constant repetition of the word *moral* sometimes gets lost in English translation. Could a man who made this kind of bitter fun of himself and his own ideas successfully lead a republican state caught up in a desperate civil war? Moreover, Azaña, as author, allows other characters to challenge successfully his characters Garcés and Morales, and he gives the last word to Pastrana, the Socialist.

Other participants in the dialogue speak words and ideas of people with whom Azaña had recently talked. He says this in his preface, and anything else would be quite out of character with the whole work. Notations by his friend Carlos Montilla indicate that the lawyer, Marón, speaks of the Model Prison massacre using words that Angel Ossorio, also a Catholic and a lawyer, spoke to Azaña on that occasion. Pastrana phrases his final attack on Morales in a way that caused Montilla to identify him, here, with Indalecio Prieto. A reference in Azaña's memoirs suggests that the frightened visitor with an unpublished manuscript has something in him of the historian Claudio Sánchez Albornoz, but he also suggests Azaña's relationship with Salvador de Madariaga, who had served as Spain's delegate on the Council of the League of Nations. How much does Barcala, the propagandist, speak as Largo Caballero? Does Doctor Lluch represent Juan Negrín, Largo's successor as prime minister? Did Azaña's friend, the actress Margarita Xirgu, provide something of Paquita? Of course. However, we stand on solid ground in accepting the author's statement that he did not model his characters on specific personalities. At most they represent composites.

Four of Azaña's characters talk about the war as a personal adventure: Rivera, the somewhat naive former millionaire; Lluch, a disillusioned scientist; Blanchart, the Loyalist army officer, devoted to discipline and duty; and Paquita Vargas, actress and Spanish woman. Along with two other soldiers, whose presence is mainly symbolic, Paquita and Rivera provide the voice of the people, common sense, which cuts through clouds of discussion by the intellectuals at key points. Notably, only Rivera and Pastrana stay with the discussion to its end. Barcala comes closest of all to being a straw man, useful mainly to provide a target for the others; he makes some points but not many.

Four other characters turn the civil war, in all of its historical complexity and heartrending presence, into a dialogue of ideas. Garcés and Morales soon agree about the war's futility; indeed, Manuel Aragón, the book's most recent editor, has noted that they do not really disagree about anything. Pastrana, though allowed to put down Morales, finishes by augmenting his opponent's most pessimistic projections. Marón takes a different tack; he is the hardest character to place. Aragón calls him Azaña's Pangloss, but this somewhat misses his character. Marón stands for the old Spain. Like Barcala, he speaks in platitudes, but his platitudes represent the kind of thinking on which traditional Spain rested. As Barcala stands closest to the radicals among the Benicarló disputants, so Marón, even more than the Spartan Blanchart, serves as a republican representative of the kind of men who served with Franco.

Flavored with a crushing pessimism induced by a war that was going badly, the discussion ranges through various problems that obsessed men in the mid-twentieth century. Participants have ambivalent feelings about revolution, for instance. The Second Republic, like other republics in Europe and America, owed its existence to what its opponents regarded as revolution. Now in 1937 an open army rebellion,

[23]

a veritable revolution, challenged this Republic. At the same time, and far more confusing to a liberal conscience, internal revolution weakened the Republic, seeking to engulf it or to break free from it. In a general way the dialogue's supporters of this continuing revolution identify it with social, socialistic reform, but in fact it had many facets, including anarchism, Catalan and Basque nationalism, and a seeming infinity of personal and local interests all contending against each other.

Searching for some clear and absolute sanction for their Republic, and for their own ideas, Azaña's characters appeal to the people's will. He fully recognized the responsibility of the anonymous voter, the mere newspaper reader, and, notably, of women. Yet at the same time he recognized both a basic, possibly inevitable, irresponsibility in popular attitudes and their corrupting influence on politicians who sought popular approval. The state needed a higher standard than mere popular endorsement. This involved Azaña in a search for a secularist-liberal absolute. Throughout the dialogue, even more than with *revolution,* he plays with the word *moral,* which in Spanish pertains to moral attitudes and ethics as well as to morale.

Ultimately, for Azaña, the Republic must sink its roots in nationality and national tradition; he finally appealed to history. His repeated insistence on the facts of history, as opposed to theory, is significant. However, what he found in the historical Spanish national character did not reassure him. He found his countrymen traditionally intolerant, fanatical, and highly individualistic: in short, not easily adaptable to the kind of republic he hoped for. Like his character Morales and his mentors of the Generation of '98, Azaña saw the best hope for Spain's future achievement in the civilizing mission of her artistic and intellectual creativeness. Education might reshape Spaniards. Thus, in the midst of military and political crisis, he himself undertook to write *Vigil in Benicarló.*

Nonetheless, it remained the special mission of Azaña's generation to go beyond this through political action; indeed, the wave of violence that swept over Spain and all of Europe after the First World War left them no choice. Without their active leadership on the national level, even intellectual achievement would become submerged. He refers to the postwar generation "which disdains intelligence, neglects study, and, instead, cultivates physical strength and personal insolence." Azaña's crushing pessimism, then, comes not only from a war that was going badly, even including his personal problems; it is rooted in the philosophical-historical dilemma of his generation. Blanchart and Lluch, his obvious heroes in the book, are existentialists who go on with their work without illusions. Among the principal characters, Pastrana does not stand far from them.

In the spring of 1937 Spain and Europe were living through an extraordinary moment when a century's problems came into clear focus, a great historical parable of twentieth-century Western civilization. *Vigil in Benicarló* presents Azaña's view of the larger scene. It remains a limited view, Spain's particular experience of the general nightmare, a rational voice commenting on an irrational world. His two most obvious spokesmen respond to unreasonable propaganda by refusing point-blank to go on with the discussion. Nonetheless, training and experience had prepared him extraordinarily well to speak for his position and his nation. Furthermore, he transcends any impression of the dialogue as merely his own internal debate, and gives force to his arguments, by insisting on historical fact—for him the ultimate proof. Deliberately, he makes his dialogue part of the real world in which it took place. On two occasions he presents his own ideas directly by having characters quote recent speeches of the president of the Republic. The Ciempozuelos of Garcés's fable did lie between the two armies; destruction threatened the Prado Museum, in fact. The famous and infamous bombardment of Guernica occurred while Azaña was working on this manuscript. Ultimately his dialogue stands, like Picasso's masterpiece, *Guernica,* as a commentary on sudden, violent, personally meaningless death, which provided the period with its most characteristic theme.

P.S.

Editions of *Vigil in Benicarló*

La Veillée à Benicarló. Translated by Jean Camp. Paris: Gallimard, 1939.

La Velada en Benicarló: Diálogo sobre la guerra de España. Buenos Aires: Editorial Losada, S.A., 1939.

La Velada en Benicarló. In *Obras completas de Manuel Azaña,* edited by Juan Marichal, 4 vols., 3:379–460. Mexico City: Editorial Oasis, S.A., 1966–68.

La Veglia a Benicarló. Translated by Leonardo Sciascia and Salvatore Girgenti. Milan: Einaudi, 1967.

La Velada en Benicarló. Edited by Manuel Aragón. Madrid: Editorial Castalia, 1974.

Sources for the Translator's Introduction

Marichal has written long introductions for each of the volumes of Azaña's *Obras;* his introduction to the first volume was published separately as *La Vocación de Manuel Azaña* (Mexico City, 1960). These, Azaña's own writing for the period 1936–40, and the introduction to the Sciascia and, especially, the Aragón editions of *Vigil* have been my principal sources. In addition I used the following books:

Aguado, Emiliano. *Don Manuel Azaña Díaz.* Barcelona: Ediciones Nauta, 1972.

Borkenau, Franz. *The Spanish Cockpit.* London: Faber and Faber, 1937.

Chabás, Juan. *Literatura española contemporanea, 1898–1950.* Habana: Cultural, 1952.

Cruells, Manuel. *Mayo sangriento: Barcelona 1937.* Barcelona: Editorial Juventud, 1970.

Jackson, Gabriel. *The Spanish Republic and the Civil War, 1931–1939.* Princeton: Princeton University Press, 1972.

[26]

Knoblaugh, H. Edward. *Correspondent in Spain.* New York: Sheed and Ward, 1937.

La Cruz, Francisco. *El Álzamiento, la revolución y el terror en Barcelona.* Barcelona: Librería Arysel, 1943.

Orwell, George. *Homage to Catalonia.* Boston: The Beacon Press, 1955.

Ramos Oliveira, Antonio. *Politics, Economics and Men of Modern Spain, 1808–1946.* London: Gollancz, 1946.

Rivas Cherif, Cipriano. *Retrato de un desconocido (Vida de Manuel Azaña).* Mexico: Editorial Oasis, 1961.

Sedwick, Frank. *The Tragedy of Manuel Azaña and the Fate of the Spanish Republic.* Columbus: Ohio State University Press, 1963.

Thomas, Hugh. *The Spanish Civil War.* New York: Harper and Row, 1963.

Vigil in Benicarló

Preface

I wrote this dialogue in Barcelona, two weeks before the May 1937 insurrection. I took advantage of a four-day siege provided by that event to dictate my definitive text from a rough draft. I am publishing it (not having been able to do so earlier) without adding a syllable. Whether or not the subsequent course of history corroborates the viewpoints expressed in the dialogue matters little. The book did not emerge from a fatidic seizure. It is not a prophecy. It is an exposition. In the form of an argument, it pulls together widely proclaimed opinions about the Spanish war and others hardly audible in the din of battle, but which existed and were felt deeply. Any effort to unmask my interlocutors, expecting to find well-known faces beneath their masks, would prove useless. The characters are imaginary. The opinions and so-called state of mind revealed by them are strictly authentic, verifiable even now if anyone felt it worth the trouble. They all agree in showing an aspect of Spain's drama that lies deeper and will last longer than the war's monstrous circumstances. In the future when labels have changed and many of our concepts have become meaningless, Spaniards will not quite understand why their predecessors have fought against each other for more than two years. The drama, however, will continue if the Spanish character retains its tragic capacity for violent partisanship. Seeing it once again in its full fratricidal fury has brought some persons to the depths of despair. On the other hand, it seems highly doubtful that this experience, short in time, too long in terms of its tribulations, will improve the reasonableness and judgment of many. It seems all the more important, then, that some have maintained an independence of spirit in these frenzied times. From the humane point of view this remains a consolation. From the Spanish point of view, a hope.

Dialogue

Those who speak in the dialogue:

Miguel Rivera, *member of the Cortes*
Doctor Lluch, *of the Faculty of Medicine of the University
  of Barcelona*
Blanchart, *major in the Infantry*
Laredo, *aviator*
Paquita Vargas, *of the theater*
Claudio Marón, *lawyer*
Eliseo Morales,*writer*
Garcés, *former minister*
A captain
Pastrana, *well-known Socialist*
Barcala, *propagandist*

(Doctor Lluch's automobile devours the distance between
Barcelona and Benicarló. On the hood of the car flutters a
mustard-colored pennant; on its rear window white letters
spelling "Doctor" are drowned in dust. Lluch's profession,
his duties, have enabled him to keep the use of his car, the last
remnant of his bourgeois comforts. With sarcasm he fleeting-
ly remembers that it once belonged to him. Traveling in the
front with Lluch is Miguel Rivera, a deputy, still young, just
six months ago a millionaire. In the back: Major Blanchart;

[33]

Laredo, an air force officer recovering from serious wounds; and Paquita Vargas, a musical comedy actress. Each traveling for a different purpose, Rivera has gotten them all a ride as far as Barcelona with his friend Lluch. In the decline of a March afternoon they cut across the plain of Panadés, rugged land that vomits its refuse into the sea, populated only by carob and olive trees; they pass through the fields of Tortosa and finally into La Plana. Ochers of the coast flame against blue water, the indistinct gloom of the Maestrazgo drowned in violet tints. No problems.

Then, halfway, a burial. Green-black cypresses, gilded by the setting sun, shelter a roadside cemetery. On top of the coffin a red-and-black flag; behind it the whole village in procession and a silent band of musicians. As the coffin passes Lluch raises his clenched fist in salute. Rivera is apprehensive. Clenched fists from the cortege respond. The sound of shuffling feet on the highway. Eyes peer into the car, attracted by uniforms. Further on a patrol.

"Halt! Your papers!"

Lluch shows a document hashed by sufficient signatures, rubrics, countersigns, and other marks to prove his loyalty. The head of the patrol peers hard enough to bore a hole through the folder. Lluch becomes impatient.

"Not so fast, comrade. I must be sure."

"You will be sure more quickly, comrade, if you will read in the right place."

They return it.

"You can go on. Good luck!"

"And to you . . . and a long life," Lluch exclaims, starting the car.

Rivera panics. "They are going to shoot at us."

"Bah! They aren't that bad."

Lluch enjoys speeding through tranquil fields, brought to elegance and fruitfulness by centuries of labor. White cottages surrounded by copper-colored, recently plowed farm land, and fresh seedlings, shining green succulence of the promised harvest. Workers' carts with arched canvas tops; their mules have harnesses bedecked with gilded studs. An occasional

[34]

vinedresser is finishing his pruning. With the flight of the car, premature flowers, miraculous brush strokes, on early fruit trees seem to come free and fly to the horizon of hoary mountains.

"They will destroy it all," Lluch murmurs. "Neither houses nor trees will remain. They've shot men. Why not women and children? We have already seen them blown to pieces. Our own turn will come. . . ."

Impressionable Rivera usually yielded to others' opinions; his own recent and ominous experience made him especially sensitive to frightening predictions. Yet he wanted to find proof of his luck in that experience, as if he had exhausted all adverse possibilities.

"I have saved my skin from so many dangers that I believe I am destined to survive."

Lluch replies, "Saving your life once doesn't guarantee it forever. Don't confuse your romantic adventures with real danger. They give you no advantage. Destiny doesn't always reveal itself so obviously; one dies stupidly without knowing why. Months ago I used to see dead men, soaked in their own blood, in the ditches along this road. They got hit after dinner or while they slept. Who did it? Why? When our turn comes, we also will show up as two statistics, without any real explanation of what happened. The world is finished with men like us; we are in oversupply everywhere. The elimination process will go on; it doesn't much matter how. A law of history? All right. History acts stupidly, indifferent to human intelligence or contrary to it. Man can verify history, he can endure it, nothing more. Such is the grandeur of our destiny, as they say. We differ that much from a blade of grass. I envy the grass. As there is no help for it, I accept my human weakness and play my role to the last syllable."

At nightfall they stop at a seaside inn. Western coals, turning cool, leave ashy clouds. White planes of clustered village houses. Some olive trees between orchard and garden. The silhouette of Peñíscola juts up, torn from the land. Dead calm. The stones of the shore relish a transparent ripple which expands among them without noise or foam. Other travelers

[35]

at the inn welcome Miguel Rivera with surprise and joy. Conversation goes on during dinner and afterward.)

PASTRANA.   Where have you come from?

RIVERA.   From the grave.

MORALES.   That is almost believable. Everyone gave you up for dead.

RIVERA.   I'm not lying. Literally, I come from the grave. I was passing through Logroño visiting my brothers when the rebellion began. If the people had had arms they would have won, but their resistance collapsed quickly. Then what executions! They shot my brother, the artillery captain; the other, the engineer, they killed on the Zaragoza road, both merely for being republicans. Before killing them, they pulled out some gold teeth. I was able to hide. I spent four months in a shepherd's hut in the hills. In the meantime they judged me a rebel, condemned me to death, and confiscated all of our goods, including those of my mother. Now at the age of eighty she lives on charity.

A squad of soldiers found my hiding place. I thought my last hour had come. They turned out to be friends, workers from Haro, fugitives. They told me of the slaughter in La Rioja. Incredible. In the main towns all registered voters were shot. I told them who I was, and we joined forces. They put me in touch with a man who owned a car. He took me to Pamplona shut up in its trunk. The only place he could think to hide me was a cemetery. "I have a good friend here," he said. I also had many friends there, all dead. In Navarre only Carlists, Nationalists, and Catholics survived. In the elections the republican coalition got no more than thirty-six thousand votes. Well, they shot some fifteen thousand people; if that proportion holds for all of Spain, you can imagine. . . . My driver did, in fact, have a gravedigger friend. I spent twenty-four days in a tomb; I wasn't afraid my neighbors would denounce me. At night I came out to stretch my legs and get a little bread and a jug of water. My protector helped me escape. I arrived at the border on foot in a friar's robe and dragged my bones into Arnéguy. I had nothing but the skin and bones under my robe. I should not have believed that a person would suffer so much to stay alive. It took me several weeks to recover. I wanted to return to Spain. . . .

MORALES.   A strange case.

RIVERA.   I realize that now. With borrowed money I got to La Junquera. They arrested me on suspicion. I had no papers. I told them that I was a deputy and that made it worse.

PASTRANA.   Being a deputy was almost as bad as being a general, bishop, or landlord. Not so bad, though, as being a minister.

RIVERA.   Shut up in a hut, threatened by death, I managed to send a telephone message to Barcelona. That brought urgent orders for my transfer. Convinced that I was going to my execution, some thugs agreed to take me in a car, hands tied and the barrel of a pistol at the back of my neck. For twenty-four hours I stood in an underground dungeon jammed between men whose faces I could not see clearly. The same connection that helped me at the frontier now gained my freedom. I had only the rags on my back. Thanks to Doctor Lluch I got out of that predicament, and with the return of my health I have calmed down and even have some hope.

LLUCH.   You had nothing serious wrong with you. Let's call it prolonged hunger and nervous excitement, which soon took care of themselves when you had adjusted to the new life. At first you hardly knew where you were. As if you had fallen from the moon.

RIVERA.   For almost half a year I knew nothing about Spain except the shooting of thousands of men and women in La Rioja and Navarre. Nothing else. I arrived in Barcelona imagining myself the protagonist of an exceptional drama. Prolonged hunger . . . no doubt. But, believe me, I needed to get the load off my mind more than I needed food and a change of clothes, at least to talk to someone about it all. I needed warmth, compassion. Your reception was glacial. I just had no conception of what you had gone through day after day, or that you could no longer feel amazement or pity about anyone. I fell into a new city. I had escaped death only to become part of a society which also lived with a pistol at the back of its neck. That strange impression of our first meeting remains fresh, Lluch. What a lot I expected to tell you! You met me with these words: "Hello, Rivera! What brings you to Barcelona?" I was dumbfounded. And without a pause you added, "So you're letting your beard grow?" Remember and laugh; now I can laugh at myself. I thought I walked into your house a tragic character. In fact I was just an unshaven young gentleman. Suddenly everything I wanted to tell you seemed ridiculous.

LLUCH.   You asked about the dog. When I told you that an automobile had killed it, you screamed out, "The dog, too, the dog, too!" Then, I confess, I thought that you were out of your head.

RIVERA.   The indifference everywhere disconcerted me because I didn't understand. In fact, from the time I crossed the border I should have realized that things had changed. Even worse, some people envied me because I had been in a foreign country, yet at the same time they pitied me because I had returned. I had returned to Spain quite naturally, unhesitatingly. A Barcelona acquaintance said to me, "What! You came back here from France? It would have been a cold day when I came back!" I felt furious. I had done my duty, and they made a fool of me. Perhaps out of fury, or contagious fear, or just not wanting to appear foolish, I began to wonder whether I ought not to leave. Lluch dissuaded me.

LLUCH.   Let's get it straight. I have always carefully avoided telling anyone what to do, excepting my patients, and even there suspecting that they won't do it. Because you asked, I told you that I didn't think you faced any special danger. You hadn't saved the life of any archbishop or monk. You had no connection with Catalonia's political and social tangles; in fact you haven't harmed or helped anyone in my land. But I didn't say that you should go away or stay. I refuse to assume responsibility for anyone's destiny.

[38]

MORALES.   You assume responsibility equally whether you give advice or refrain from it.

LLUCH.   Of course. But one can't go beyond omission or inaction.

MORALES.   One writer thinks he is rendering great service through his rather obvious flight from Spain.

MARÓN.   So I have heard. An example of how judgment and good taste are badly distributed among men. Men who really care about public opinion are always driven toward swaying the gullible; they always try to please everyone. In their own way, though, these men who prefer hunger to fear may really be heroes. They may really be doing the right thing by leaving, because hunger merely weakens whereas fear drives men crazy. Where hunger incites crime, fear incites depravity. The worst bargain, though, is to suffer hunger after having yielded already to fear. I myself don't care about popularity.

MORALES.   Perhaps we shouldn't judge so severely. Looking ahead, men who have withdrawn from present horrors will stand as a peacetime reserve.

LLUCH.   I seem to hear their voices. Two months ago the government sent me to buy medical supplies in Paris. I ran into a Barcelona friend, a big shot in Catalan politics who had emigrated in the first days of the war. "How are you getting along with the FAI?" he burst out. "We're waiting for you to come back and finish it off," I answered. He explained the scheme to which you refer. Two ferocious parties are trying to destroy each other in Spain. Neither can dominate the other. When everyone recognizes this and the war comes to an end, those who remained far away and condemned both parties all along will take charge of governing the country. I make no attempt to hide my horror about many things happening on both sides in this war, but hearing this foolishness sent the intransigent spirit of a militiaman surging through my veins.

MARÓN.   By my count at least four Spains already exist. In

Paris they had formed a third Spain, that of your Barcelona friend. But now a fourth Spain has sprung up with much better schemes. They only need to get into a civil war in Paris like the first two in the Peninsula.

Really, all of these honorary members of the Nonintervention Committee are having bad luck. If the war had ended in September with the Republic's destruction, they would always have remained disillusioned but at peace with themselves. "You see? It was all lost anyhow! What could we do?" Prolongation of an indecisive war must annoy them, in spite of themselves, because it leaves them in an awkward position with no possible excuse. Just being there is harmful, even though they remain silent (and not all of them do remain silent). When they talk . . . their least harmful subject is self-justification for the energy they are wasting in carefully working out their projects that could only succeed with saints.

PASTRANA.   Oh yes. They are far superior to us savages who have to live through bombings. You can see it when they happen to come to Spain. One of them was in Valencia for four days. Much annoyed because the government didn't expedite the publication of his book on Receswinth. That's right, Receswinth! He talked to me about the Foreign Office, the *Quai d'Orsay*, the Gentlemen's Agreement, the Covenant of the League, about collective security, the settlement of Assyrian peasants, the Conference of Nine, the Committee of Twenty-three. . . . Fending off a reproach that didn't even occur to me, he adopted a casual loftiness. I read a kind of distant, compassionate protectiveness in his eyes. That night we suffered an air raid. Much noise. Some died. The man turned up at my house asking me to obtain an exit permit for him from Prieto on the first plane out. I didn't hit him. He has crossed the Pyrenees. My laughter still follows him.

GARCÉS.   They have already acknowledged defeat. With that kind of morale what can you expect?

MARÓN.   Not defeat in the war? That still remains up in the air.

GARCÉS. Defeat by social cataclysm.

MARÓN. Spanish society is not done for either. Let's admit that it will change. But won't you and I still be part of it?

MORALES. A person can't base morale on his own particular circumstances, not morale that has any general relevance. This is true whether the morale anticipates defeat or victory. Defeatist morale is as useless for bearing defeat as for attaining victory. Morale based on certainty of victory isn't much more useful. If victory doesn't come in the end, a man is left with nothing but degrading pusillanimity. Even if victory does come this kind of morale doesn't prove very useful for handling it. After all, in its own way victory enervates and corrupts as much as defeat. On the other hand, informed men ought not to remain, as the saying goes, in the middle of the road, suspending their judgments about external events like war or revolution no matter how clamorous or excessive or terrible they may become. For self-discipline I refuse to worry about defeat or victory. Morale must remain a matter of intelligence rather than of fortitude, and it has to superimpose itself on all contingencies, including these two. It matters very much whether we win or lose the war, but that is not the key to our suffering. Not even from a political viewpoint. Not,needless to say, in our personal moral orientation!

PASTRANA. My friend, you sound like a budding emigrant.

MORALES. And you are giving me a bad time, as always.

PASTRANA. A thousand pardons. I only wanted to say that I don't agree with you.

LLUCH. I do agree, if I have understood correctly. At least as to method. . . . I also try to surmount contingencies. I don't base what you call my morale on personal preferences, nor on my first reaction to events, nor on what I hope or fear about their outcome. I've not had adventures like those of our friend Rivera. I hardly believe that I've faced the danger of death. I have attended the deaths of many others. I serve by performing my duty as a doctor in relieving suffering. A field

[41]

hospital is a school that inculcates old-fashioned ideas, ideas inapplicable in real life, unfortunately. But that's something else. I try to catch a glimpse of what awaits me as a man and to face it serenely. It satisfies me just to understand and, if I can, to label things. I hear talk of traitor generals, of homicidal anarchists, of bloody Falangists. . . . This doesn't quite hit the mark. It's all true, but merely anecdotal.

MARÓN. Blasphemy!

LLUCH. No. Fever is an inconvenience or a threat to a patient's life, not a basic malfunction of his constitution. Similarly what is going on today doesn't conform to our usual political concepts. Or do you believe that liberty, social order, justice, etcetera have universal bloodbath as their premise or bear it as their fruit? But forget about politics. Our problem is that man is a more intelligent animal than a dog or a monkey, but an animal. Man doesn't hunger for liberty. Human life doesn't feed on justice. Order, or call it the tranquillity of the fortunate, rests on the misfortune of the poor. To the degree that we allow the idea of justice to dazzle us, we denounce oppression and are outraged by misery. But what is this justice that no one has ever achieved? An offspring of the human mind. Man embellishes his horrifying bestiality with cunning inventions. Christianity's fundamental pessimism remains irrefutable. It puts justice in another world. What sarcasm! Today's passing phase of accelerated destruction represents a relapse, not a malfunction.

I confront the plain facts and evaluate them. I reject all dialectical apparatus that tries to classify events by fitting them into a system, even though it may well become tomorrow's system of political history. In searching for an explanation, even a justification, why must we argue on the basis of inadequate concepts or false analogies? In another age they called a plague or an invasion the scourge of God. It used to be argued that man's great wickedness, as viewed from the other world, justified his destruction. His sin: the involuntary one of his birth. The precedent: the Flood. Does your reasoning move you to substitute some other earthly or supernatural concept of justice for all that? Not even the Spanish archbishops have gone so far as to call our current calamity Heaven's punishment.

GARCÉS.   They do pray to God to help the rebels.

LLUCH.   That's just politics.

MARÓN.   Your sarcasm sounds bitter.

LLUCH.   I have given up sarcasm completely, like tobacco. At first I found a refuge from my disgust in laughing at all the stupidity and wickedness; I began to relish it as a kind of retaliation. Then one day I realized that I had gone too far, and since then I have made a major effort to control myself. My defense was worth about as much as taking morphine or getting drunk. Since my return from the front I have worked in a Barcelona hospital under the supervision of a committee of its lower-echelon officials. I haven't found out whether the committee includes a delegation of patients, but after all, who has a better right! Remembering a recent difficulty with an unscrupulous patient, I laughed, out of the wrong side of my mouth, considering the possible consequences of any professional decision. "What if I make a mistake sometime?" I thought. "If a sick person dies in my hands, they may call me a traitor and say that I have deprived the Republic of a soldier. From now on I had better submit any possible amputation of a leg to a committee vote." When this notion crossed my mind, I realized that laughter had become grimace. Trying to preserve my rationality, I was in the process of losing it.

As a cure I have stopped paying attention to daily events. I don't read newspapers; I don't listen to the radio; I don't keep track of politics or the war. I work like an ox; there is no possible deception in that. Thus little by little I have recovered true interior freedom, and I have sketched a brief forecast of our destiny. I see forsaken men, hundreds of thousands of them, turned into their own executioners, pushed to their deaths. I see the shipwreck of both the aggressors and their victims. The same ebb tide carries them all away. Bodies, many bodies, in waves of blood. I see this in

[43]

the innermost depths of my being. If a ship on the high seas suddenly bursts into flames at both ends, with no possible aid available, what is the use of going crazy in search of rescue?

MARÓN. The storm will pass; the sun will come out, and all the grief will not have been in vain.

LLUCH. You people argue in offices, in newspapers, in courts. I come from the hospital and the war. From their appearances, others here present come from the same places. But their judgment doesn't count for more than mine. Don't misunderstand. As soldiers they have had different training. I'm not a soldier, but a man lost in the suffering of others. You talk about the usefulness of slaughter! You sound like devotees of the ancient Hebrew God who crushes men like grapes in a tub for His own glory, with their blood splattering His thighs. In view of the urgency with which men are killing each other, I try to discover a point at which they may hope to have achieved their purpose or glory and the killing can stop. I don't find it. In the early years of this century an author wrote that the curing of Spain would require "a meter of blood." A meter? We will have more than that. If that author was right, Spain will recover. He himself died without bleeding on Spanish soil. No doubt he now rests happily in his nice dry grave. I don't believe that this bloodletting is what he had in mind, or that the country will come out of it cured.

No more sarcasm, irony, joking, scorn for me. Even "resignation" doesn't quite describe the hopeless courage that sustains me in the face of such horror. I have two props. First, the finality of the war's outcome, whether it comes today or tomorrow. Second, we are moving together in pursuit of a common destiny; everyone will share it. Consideration of a personal case, mine or someone else's, becomes pointless. That is why I gave you such a lukewarm reception, Rivera. You and I and all the rest lose our identity in the mass who march together to execution.

RIVERA. Tell these gentlemen about your unscrupulous patient.

[44]

LLUCH.   One of many such cases. Six or seven years ago I
operated on a laborer in the Clinic. A difficult amputation; I
saved his life, but it left him incapacitated. I forgot all about
it. A few days after the revolt began, he appeared with full
military gear—rifle, pistol, and a bicolored cap. He asked for
an indemnity of twenty-five thousand duros because my lack
of skill had crippled him. I made the mistake of treating it as a
joke. The thought flashed through my mind, "If all discontented patients start doing this, we doctors will really feel the
pinch. But who knows! Maybe this is justice, and it only
bothers me because I'm not used to it." Other masqueraders
soon visited me, and like it or not, they took me to a convent,
now transformed into a prison. The invalid wrote up a claim,
and I remained a hostage.

Later I found out that my younger brother, also a doctor,
went to the prison for my release. "No Lluch here," they told
him. He went around to all the jails, old and newly
improvised. He learned nothing. He talked with the authorities. "Everything will be arranged." "But where is he?"
"We don't know." "They have killed him." "They want
money, and if they kill him they won't get it." My brother
believed that I had been killed; he panicked, wanted to run
away. He tried to reach the frontier by back roads. A patrol
ordered him to halt; he ran. . . . They shot him dead. In the
meantime the authorities did their utmost to save me. A
relation of the chief of police, on good terms with the
organization that patronized the claimant, handled the bargaining: for five thousand duros everything would be settled
and they would set me free. "I will pay it if I still have enough
in my account." The mediator had the kindness and the skill
to persuade my abductors not to pursue the escapade further.
I paid and returned to my home. Several weeks later I found
out about my brother.

BLANCHART.   On what fronts did you work?

LLUCH.   Always in northern Aragon. They took me out of
Barcelona to utilize my services and also to protect me. This
suited me because it freed me from university involvements.

A sign on the facade proclaims its transformation into the University of Catalonia. These days we are more nationalistic than ever. A committee of beadles and lower-echelon employees, under the rector's nominal presidency, had charge of purging the professoriate. I didn't want to get involved in all that. Some tenured professors who opposed the regime lost their jobs; others opposed to science remained. In spite of a freeze on hiring administrative staff, they increased to a hundred and thirty employees, many more than the professors. Well, anyhow, I got away from all that. Now they are reviving the purge. The first round didn't go far enough, and they want me to take part in it. Accusations: "Don So-and-So said this or that; Beadle So-and-So kept some of his tips; he has a photograph of So-and-So in his house. . . ."

The front suited me better. I organized field hospitals and did a tour of duty in them. Afterward they transferred me to another hospital farther back from the lines in a small, ugly, barbaric city, ravaged by war and revolution. The hospital's waiting room seemed the least sad place there. What a strange experience!

GARCÉS.   Was libertarian Communism functioning there?

LLUCH.   No, sir, not during my time. It would have represented an improvement if anything had functioned. Much of the population had disappeared, all of the money. They divided provisions with traditional inequality, but now different persons got the larger shares. Great confusion, much good will, overwhelming fear. Where before one person performed a service mediocrely or badly, now seven, twelve, or twenty were determined to do it very well by talk. Those who still had no reason to feel frightened seemed insolent, overbearing, proud, like kids with new shoes. As if by magic they had their hands on the apex of the world, and they felt inclined to change its course.

The population flaunted the new style of sloppiness, filth, and rags. They seemed to belong to a swarthier race because young warriors let their beards grow, and these, almost all black, darkened faces. Long hair, woolly chests, rifles slung

[46]

across shoulders, romantic lunacies after the style of a century ago, barricades. Many people went along with the crowd from fear of appearing well-to-do, especially if they were or had been. No hats, berets at most. Shirts without collars; to wear a necktie would have been an act of defiance. It seemed a deed of valor for me to keep my usual style of dress. "They have adopted the new fashion with greater enthusiasm here than in Barcelona," I thought, remembering how the Ramblas looked after the capital adopted the beret and its people began to look as if all their clothes came from the same warehouse. Soldiers of the old army kept some modified vestige of regulation dress. The officers gave up their uniforms altogether and sported a new elegance, with luxuries like leather zippered jackets, little chains, and fancy ornaments. . . . Officers found themselves in a difficult position, increasingly painful as their loyalty was tested.

Our hospital stood next to an animal barn. After a lot of quarreling with local authorities, I got it moved to a large ramshackle house near a graveyard. "Probably because of a shortage of transport," I thought, yielding to my bad mood. The new hospital went right into operation. Almost every night, late, the sound of rifle fire came from the cemetery. The first time, I asked, "What are those shots?" The three persons with me reacted differently. The first, sullen, didn't answer. The second responded with a conniving smile, "What else?" The third said, "They are shooting in the cemetery," as he might have said, "It is raining."

One night late in August, while leaning on the windowsill of my room enjoying some fresh air, I heard three volleys in the cemetery and then silence. What happened to me? I don't know. I seemed to see light flood into the dark graveyard. I could not leave the window. A little later I heard a groan. I listened. The groan came again, stronger and stronger until it became a scream, intermittent, heartrending. . . . That darkness, the silence. . . . No one answered. Lying in a heap with those already dead, the dying man cried out from fright. He had returned to a moment of life more horrible than his frustrated death. Suddenly his cry came straight to me. I

[47]

brought some hospital employees to the window. "Let's go get him, maybe we can save him!" They refused; I argued. They prevented me from doing it. Who gets involved in that kind of thing! At most we might send a message to the authorities. We did. Time passed. Pow! Pow! Two shots in the cemetery. We heard no more groaning.

MORALES.   It is the picture of all of Spain.

MARÓN.   With an important difference. In our zone people commit these atrocities in retaliation for the revolt, or for private vengeance, only because the government can't prevent them. Furthermore everyone recognizes these crimes as the result of the revolt. In territory controlled by rebels and foreigners atrocities are part of a political plan for national regeneration, and the authorities approve of them.

MORALES.   You make your point perfectly. But I, who have never held a position of command or responsibility on either side, find no consolation in it.

BLANCHART.   Why do you find the officers' position painful?

LLUCH.   Usually they arouse suspicion. This gives others a good excuse to evade any discipline that seems too hard. I wonder whether enforcement may not seem just as hard to the man who has to impose it. In practice threatened officers allay suspicion or protect themselves by letting things go. They follow the mainstream. They don't exercise command; they leave that to committees. They have discovered a new kind of military discipline; it consists in forgetting about discipline. Unless they have also found a new way of making war, we will suffer because of it. But I don't really know anything about it. You have seen much more than I and know more about all of this. Am I right?

BLANCHART.   I've seen some things. Not so much as you suppose. Since the beginning of the war I've not seen anything beyond Barcelona. I have not commanded troops; they've filed me away in an office.

MARÓN.   That's unusual, with the shortage of field officers. . . .

[48]

BLANCHART.   You would find the explanation tedious. . . . No one can doubt my loyalty to the Republic. You know, Rivera, that even before the war I had trouble because members of the cabal at Staff Office Headquarters accused me of being a Communist. The leaders of the present rebellion were labeling all republican officers Communists at that point. I was not one; I am not one now, but even if I had been one, that would not have given them the right to harass me. I performed my duties, and I continue to perform them regardless of everything. I make others perform their duties. The irony lies in the authorities doubting me and trusting others who duck low until they know how the wind blows.

MARÓN.   Do we have people like that in the army?

BLANCHART.   Oh yes! I don't want to mention names. They are swinging back and forth, as we say, while the war remains indecisive, waiting to see how things will work out between the *Generalitat* of Catalonia and the government of the Republic. I act otherwise. I am a Catalan through all four of my grandparents, a republican, and a Spanish soldier. I do not budge, and others dislike me for it. I commanded a regiment of the Madrid garrison. In July, I came on leave to my village, Saint Felix of Llobregat. Now they call it Roses of Llobregat because they have quarreled with heaven and want to anger the saint. It's just great. . . . The day rebellion broke out I went to Barcelona as quickly as possible and presented myself to the president of the *Generalitat:* "I am an army field officer, and I place myself at the disposal of Your Excellency as the representative in Catalonia of the government of the Republic." They accepted my services. Eight months in an office; not quite my line. They have more than enough office workers in the *Generalitat's* Council of Defense: seven hundred bureaucrats to organize and administer a force that even on paper, doesn't amount to forty thousand men. I have protested. Now I have high hopes of getting a field command through the army headquarters in Valencia.

RIVERA.   From what Lluch says, you are looking for an awkward position.

BLANCHART. Not necessarily; but if so, then we must change things. After all, the conduct of many officers justifies public hostility. Besides, time has passed; people will begin to recognize us as individuals, to understand why we are serving and how we have served in the past. They also understand better now the war's real needs. Did they reject a regular military force hoping that badly armed and worse commanded mobs would find enough strength to face an army through some kind of mystical inspiration from the revolution? It had inevitable consequences. It is wicked and absurd to form military columns of untrained peasants without arms or discipline, to organize them like political parties, to stir up their political enthusiasm and to pretend that they will function as an army. It has produced disasters. If the government wants a fighting army, we the soldiers must organize it and command it, sticking to the one right way of doing it.

You can't be a soldier by halves. For instance, as his regulation appearance deteriorates, a man becomes less truly a soldier. You see me in uniform. No one else in Barcelona wears it correctly. I have never abandoned it since 19 July, even off duty. Some don't see it that way. If the army had punished the first officer who abandoned regulation dress, that would have avoided many subsequent problems. This isn't just fussiness; exterior signs of discipline really do matter. In today's army discipline has become no more than a set of petty courtesies. Some soldiers show open contempt for discipline; others show their dislike by abandoning its symbols, their uniforms. Other republican officers think as I do. Others, too, very good men, just stay on the shelf. But even if no one agreed with me, I would still be right. I would also uphold my convictions to the end. Nowadays we are seeing the last of many things, the end of many breeds. I stand among them.

PASTRANA. Because of our exceptional circumstances, we must take advantage of everyone's zeal.

BLANCHART. I agree. But we must understand how to use

effectively even the most zealous. You can't conduct a field campaign the same way you take a street barricade or the Montaña Barracks. Leading armed forces requires previous training. When you lack a cadre of officers (and this is our worst problem), you must improvise new ones. But we must not adopt improvisation permanently. Above all we need to recognize the futility of giving command to men whose talents lie in political organization, persons who know nothing about leading soldiers. Blinded by their skill at improvisation, they refuse to learn anything else. Revolutionary activity, determined and useful opportunism, do not qualify a man to lead soldiers. If a cook prevents his battalion from revolting or the diver of a battleship succeeds in keeping its officers from turning their ship over to the enemy, let's reward them. But let's not make the cook into a colonel or the diver an admiral. They won't know how to do their jobs, and we will lose battalion and ship.

MARÓN.   Maybe one could find isolated cases of this sort. I don't know of them.

BLANCHART.   Maybe you aren't looking for them. I'm talking about something that prevails everywhere. I won't go so far as to call it a system because there is no system, except systematic denial of obvious truths without finding substitutes. Whether republican, monarchist, or anarchist, Spaniards always do the same foolish things. You can already see a brood of irresponsible little dictators hatching; in due course they will rebel against whatever survives of the Republic after the war. Since 1923 Spain has seen a revival of the nineteenth century's accelerated military careers. In our violent, intolerant, undisciplined country, generals under the age of sixty represent a national hazard.

MARÓN.   Many meritorious officers have adjusted to this situation; and they not only render good service themselves, but also make their badly trained subordinates render good service.

BLANCHART.   Adjusted? Of course, if you want to call it adjustment. I know of an army captain under an illiterate

[51]

peasant, the improvised commander of his unit, who ordered, "We're going to take that ridge." "Impossible." "I order you to take it." "We will all be killed." "Your trouble is that you're afraid." The captain set up the attack. They didn't take the position, but the disaster cost eighteen hundred lives, including the captain's. Do you call that adjustment? The commander of a column of soldiers on the Aragonese front assured me that in all operations in which he has participated he has always had to keep in mind both the military situation and the political situation. In other cases political commissars have refrained from giving orders and acted as what we would call adjutants to the military men who serve as their subordinates. Adjust? Sure! Some officers have so completely adjusted that they serve some factional aim rather than their military responsibilities. They think only about their popularity. Sooner or later this brings terrible disillusionment. No matter how much he compromises, in the end a military man cannot accept something professionally absurd. Then popularity changes into distrust, applause into threats. Some such men have hidden themselves away in Barcelona, fearing the vengeance of the anonymous power that they thought their submission had appeased.

MORALES. Can you take a command with this attitude, in conditions that disgust you?

BLANCHART. Yes, certainly! Anything rather than rotting among those papers. . . . My devotion to the Republic hasn't diminished, quite the contrary. I want to serve in the best way I can, from a sense of vocation and a sense of duty. Besides, what can I do apart from the military? I know how to command a battalion and lead it into combat. That's what I want. I have always loved my career. I don't have the adolescent dreams of glory for myself, for the army, or for Spain that I may have had once. I know our country's history, its poverty, its backwardness. Anyhow, the years have taught me that military glory provides a shaky base in politics. In spite of everything, though, I have always believed it possible to serve within my profession in such a way as to make a contribution. The time has come. I should prefer a less depressing occasion, but what can I do about it? I only regret that they have delayed my appointment for so many months. As there is a war, a war of invasion against the Republic, I naturally want to fight in it.

That doesn't make me a warmonger. I like my career, but I have never desired to convert my officer's commission into a license for piracy. Keeping within the limits of professionalism requires that you moderate your ambitions and even, to a degree, control your spirit. I certainly measure up there. Few of us military men come from Catalonia; Catalan youth chooses independent, lucrative professions. I am a soldier because my father was one. He enlisted to fight the Carlists and came out a colonel. Twenty years in the army have removed many of my illusions. Nevertheless the profession has provided me with the bases of my moral life: stimulus for good conduct, a corrective for my tendency to be headstrong, food for my capacity for work. My reputation makes me authoritarian and uncompromising. They give me nicknames because I make others serve, because I don't allow service to become servility. The delay in my employment suggests the indelibility of these old blemishes.

MARÓN.   There aren't many like you.

BLANCHART.   There are more than you think. I'm not ruled by wartime political fanaticism like the majority in both camps. The minority with a little common sense find themselves blocked; maybe others feel obliged to hide their good sense for the present. Men like me also serve in the rebel camp. Sometimes I think about them. How will they feel if the rebellion triumphs, dependent on German and Italian armies, not to mention the Moroccans? When these people, called in because of the rebellion's weakness, have taken control of Spain, will their generals withdraw, merely extending good wishes? "Well, we have conquered the Peninsula for you. It's all yours. Enjoy it." No. Before the final bill is settled, some of my former comrades will join me in that corner of the cemetery where they bury those who die of shame.

GARCÉS.   Nothing that you say indicates that you have

[53]

failed to adapt yourself. Quite the contrary. We have suffered some very costly losses, unnecessary from an orthodox viewpoint, because we've violated established rules. But theory must always yield to fact. The element of surprise was very important in the state's breaking up, and our army went first of all. Things are coming together again now, and these values that you uphold will prevail first in the military.

CAPTAIN. If only it's not too late! I saw a very serious example of that excessive adjustment you mentioned, sir, in Málaga.

MARÓN. So! You were in Málaga.

CAPTAIN. Until four days before the city fell. I got hit by shrapnel. Nothing, fifteen days in the hospital. . . . Luckily they evacuated me. We had an incredible military commander: "I don't build fortifications," he said, "I sow revolution. If factions appear, the revolution will swallow them up." That was how he prepared the defense of an endangered city full of internal revolt. It's a wonder they didn't take it sooner. A pushover. Debarkation at Estepona cost them nothing. What could we use against them— revolution? In Málaga we had six guns and seven or eight thousand rifles to cover a fifty-kilometer front. Why we had no more weapons is another story. We heard rumors. . . . Certainly the government lacked troops and matériel. And Málaga seemed a long way off! Another point. They had thousands of tons of oil stored there, worth millions. The government wanted to remove it. What committee, what bureaucrat, what governor, or what junta for defense refused to act? The Italians got the oil.

MARÓN. Was that unbelievable man in charge really an army commander?

CAPTAIN. He still is.

BLANCHART. Men like that have done much harm. Popularity at any price! They have convinced the masses that this is what it means to be a soldier of the Republic or of the revolution.

[54]

RIVERA.   No. The people ask only for loyalty. If some charlatans have tried to build up a clientele through publicity and distortion, that's something else. Have the people ever bothered you? Have they offended you?

BLANCHART.   The government's indifference has offended me.

RIVERA.   That's also something else. To make my point: I witnessed the scene in a Barcelona café where you played a part.

BLANCHART.   An involuntary part.

RIVERA.   It means more because of that. I was sitting in the café with Paquita and other friends, near a window. A Cadillac drove up, flying a red-and-black pennant, with the initials FAI on its doors. Five husky men stepped out, hardly more than boys. Breeches, leggings, leather jackets and caps, pistols, rifles. . . . They sat down unnoticed at a table. Later we saw Blanchart with Laredo, who was still on crutches. As they approached the entrance, a woman selling newspapers came forward. Do you remember what she said, Blanchart?

BLANCHART.   She said, "I'm pleased to open the door for two loyal soldiers."

RIVERA.   Exactly. Then while you threaded your way through the tables in the café, looking for us, people stopped talking. Someone got up and raised his clenched fist, in salute. Others imitated him, and in a few seconds everyone was up, excepting the armed youths who didn't seem to notice your entry.

PASTRANA.   The charisma of a wounded aviator.

MARÓN.   Seriously wounded, apparently.

LAREDO.   These things just happen.

PAQUITA.   Don't you believe it! The poor man, badly crippled, had to go on foot, and those bums in the Cadillac wasting gasoline.

LAREDO.   I'll be flying again in a month.

MARÓN (to Lluch). Is something going on between those two?

LLUCH (to Marón). So far, I give up all hope for Rivera. You can guess the rest.

BARCALA. How long have you been in Barcelona?

PAQUITA. Three months. An air raid burned us out of our theater in Madrid. Horrible! Some friends brought me to Barcelona. I went around to the CNT and got work.

MORALES. In old Barcelona
Before the hidalgos
Paquita the gypsy
Danced her fandangos.
The vision of a romantic poet.

RIVERA. Paquita is no gypsy.

PAQUITA. Me? Come on!

RIVERA. Nor does she dance fandangos.

MORALES. Then all of my hypotheses collapse.

BARCALA. Don't you have a contract yet?

PAQUITA. If you call it a contract! Some help! Everyone the same, three duros a performance, stagehand and lead soprano. A full house, but three duros. It comes from being collectivized. They take in more than twenty thousand duros every day from theaters and movies, and they don't give us anything. Nobody complains. One night I caused a scandal because I refused to repeat my number. Let the stagehand repeat it. Don't we get paid the same? But everyone puts up with it. Have you seen *The Vagabond Millionaire* at the movie theater on the Paseo de San Juan? It's very topical these days.

RIVERA. I've seen *Lives in Danger*, which seems just as topical.

PAQUITA. I'm devoted to the Republic, but all this. . . .

BARCALA. You're something even better than a republican. I'd become a Fascist for you. . . .

PAQUITA.   Idiot! Of course you have to be a Fascist these days to get a piece of the pie. Look at Teresita San Juan and her husband in Barcelona. They don't work. They go to the *Generalitat* asking for permission to sail to America, and it supports them. Crummy Carlists. They could never stand the Republic. Snobs from *Blanco y Negro.* . . . Now they suck up to those in control. They'll get their passage to America, and when they get there they'll tear us to pieces, like Soledad Martínez did. She took off from here, after getting everything she wanted. What has she said in Havana? Horrible things. It will be the same with Teresita. They don't learn. Antonia de Gracia is with her. . . . You know her, Miguel. You ought to hear the things she says about you all! She acts like a marquesa who has lost her chapel and her olive orchards. Why don't you complain to the government about it?

RIVERA.   If they have no money or are terribly afraid, why haven't they just gone away like the former ministers? Let them go to blazes. Just so the revolution doesn't get to the point where I have to watch their performances.

PAQUITA.   You are all the same. You do nothing. I don't love you any more, Miguel.

RIVERA.   Woman's intransigence!

MARÓN.   A redoubtable force. If Paquita insists on your denouncing Paquita, you will denounce her. No, no! Don't be angry, Paquita, It is only a manner of speaking. No one can quarrel with what you say. I meant to speak in general terms. Have you people reckoned the part played by women in the origins of this war—I mean the rebellion? Women feel political passions even more violently than men. They curb themselves less because with their inferior educations they don't realize the consequences of what they do.

In 1931 a middle-class lady said, "We women should thank the Republic because in giving us the vote it has converted us from objects into citizens." A rare opinion among ladies. They had the right to vote. For the orderly development of Spanish politics we preferred that opposition be vented through voting. But most ladies don't value their vote. In

[57]

fact, they despise it; they don't need it, and in some ways it doesn't suit their self-interest. A lady understands that numerically her vote will always count less than those of her maids. Still more, she realizes that her greatest personal power lies within the family and social ambience. Women have had very powerful, if inconspicuous influence in Spanish public life. So powerful that by merely channeling it into voting they would come out losing. I don't particularly refer to well-known Amazons who controlled influential husbands from the hearthside under both monarchy and Republic. No, quite generally in that stratum of the bourgeoisie, which at least gives lip service to moderate liberalism, women have had enormous influence, sometimes decisive. It comes from the fact that this stratum of Spanish society provides most of the government personnel.

As a lawyer I've become familiar with the inner workings of many families, and I have seen frequent enough examples to make it clear that they are not exceptional. Many Spanish men just don't have firm control of their families. Many maintain a kind of Moorish domination in their marriage, believing themselves the masters. They would consider it degrading to stand on an equal footing with their wives. "How can you think that my wife . . . !" "I will not tolerate . . . !" Apparently relegating her to care of the household, taking pride in her when she looks pretty, they maintain what they call the Spanish tradition. Women themselves don't mind it, especially among the bourgeoisie where freedom of behavior remains more restricted and fear of scandal prevails more than in the upper class. However, women bide their time and, excepting the stupid and frivolous, they take revenge for so unfair a situation in important matters, not just in matters of dress and amusement. When the religious beliefs or political preferences of husband and wife differ (something frequent in the middle class), household peace depends on the husband's submission, no matter how much he pretends otherwise. Therefore I assert, paradoxically, that in the long run equality of rights for men and women, or "the legal and political emancipation of

[58]

women," will bear an unexpected fruit. Husbands will come to exercise an independence and freedom of action all too infrequently achieved in the past.

With children, woman's domination projects into the future. Mother love lends her greater ardor in preserving her children from dangers that make her shudder. She fancies that her country's society should be an enlarged projection of her own household. Here the connection with politics becomes immediate and obvious. The agnosticism usually adopted by Catholics who lose their faith and the need for domestic peace increase a wife's influence. Sons of Voltaireans become pupils of the Jesuits.

This helps to explain why the Spanish bourgeoisie, born from a liberal revolution in the last century, has not yet succeeded in establishing a great social tradition. It has never thoroughly controlled the government, nor governed on the basis of its own aims and doctrines. In fact, it has not superseded the powers against which it originally rebelled—crown, army, and the political tutelage of Rome. Many remain loyal to the king, although their ardor may have lessened. These people submit easily to dictatorship, and from their ranks come those who have made Catholicism a political program. . . . Monstrous nonsense! As a bourgeois and a Catholic, I condemn it. Covering a strictly political and social quarrel with the banner of religion both splits the bourgeoisie and discredits religion. We can thank women for this stress on religious crusading that many enemies of the Republic have given to our war. First, because this is how they envision it; most of them see nothing else in it. Second, it represents a bow in their direction to keep them favorably disposed.

MORALES.   After all that, what part did women play in the rebellion's origin?

MARÓN.   Oh, yes. I got lost in my own argument. They have helped to create a climate favorable to violence when votes alone couldn't bring down the government. Many women openly encouraged those charged with bringing off the rebellion. We have freedom of speech; they had the right to express their irritations about politics. But I have heard too many ladies saying to military men things like "Are you going to tolerate this? What is the army going to do? When will it act?" They didn't realize the seriousness of their influence; most of them have forgotten their imprudent words, or have regretted them now that they are suffering through their loved ones. Without realizing what they were doing, they pushed their husbands and sons to their deaths. I don't blame them; I feel sorry for them. Let ignorance stand as their excuse. A military coup seemed easy to them, as harmless and splendid as a military parade.

MORALES. Perhaps we misjudge women's real feelings about this war. In any case, it seems unjust to me, or if you prefer, inexact, to ascribe their rancor to spitefulness or simple ignorance. I know a very benevolent bourgeois lady in Valencia, incapable of hurting a fly. When we talked in her presence about atrocities the rebels had committed in Seville, this lady would say, compassionately, "Yes, yes. They have had to exact very severe punishment."

PAQUITA. And you didn't answer her?

MORALES. Much good it would have done!

PAQUITA. The other side shoots our people when they talk like that.

MORALES. True, but we aren't on the other side. I cite this example because the feminine mind to which you have referred has very deep roots, perhaps as deep as the feminine heart. You'll find it much less analytical, less political than man's mind, but harder to influence through reasoning and prudence. Women of this temper can hold their tongues if circumstances require it, but don't expect them to change their minds on the basis of argument. You could more easily convince one of the rebelling generals. Purely feminine passions have noticeably fed the fires of this war: irritated stubbornness, frenzy, irreconcilable resentment. Possibly certain traits of the Spanish character have found a special

[60]

sanctuary in woman's heart, so that she shows them in more undiluted form than man. "More papist than the pope. . . . Throw in the rope after the bucket. . . . Support without compromise. . . ." These expressions of diverse origins, some coined to signify masculine honor, reveal lack of proportion and excessive pride in action. Woman understands and applies them more instinctively than man. We must agree with Marón that experience does not weaken the feminine will. Of all of us here, no one is more . . . how shall I say it? . . . more forceful than our charming Paquita.

PAQUITA.   It doesn't take much for that.

BARCALA.   How does ignorance excuse the women who, according to you, fomented the military rebellion?

MARÓN.   It excuses them from deliberately inciting something cruel. Victory seemed easy and almost instantaneous. The prospect of a brutal civil war might have restrained them, as it did many others. At least leave me this illusion.

BARCALA.   Even with an instantaneous and bloodless triumph like that of 1923, no one could have failed to foresee cruel repression like that going on now in provinces that offered no resistance to the rebellion. Anticipating this cruelty should have been enough to restrain them. Or does civil war seem frightening because it hurts everyone equally and repression not seem frightening because it hurts only enemies?

PASTRANA.   Why this whim to classify political sentiments according to sexual differences? Why this special preoccupation with women? Males and females on both sides have highly diverse sentiments. We should grade shades of opinion in terms of the totality of each side, not by grouping sopranos on one side and baritones and basses on the other like a choral society.

GARCÉS.   Exactly. The soul's temper has little or nothing to do with sex. The heat of fear has incubated this rebellion. The bogeyman of social revolution, manipulated by antirepublican propagandists, disturbed the sleep of many peaceful persons. In fact it was a bogeyman, but Spanish people remain somewhat childish in their political understanding. We erred in treating its demoralizing effect as a joke.

Add, especially in regard to women, horror about the laic laws. These made them believe in the extirpation of religion and the reign of the Antichrist, a belief shared, authorized, by some males of stature who were sick with worry. Believers continued to hear mass, receive sacraments, and attend public acts of worship; the clergy enjoyed freedom to attack public authority in a way that the monarchy never allowed. Yet many, women especially, believed the illusions of their imaginations more than their direct daily experience. Just human nature. Rarely does a person see clearly what occurs around him. Crowds never do. In our climate of visionaries the ability to see things directly ceases to seem a virtue and may even become a hindrance. My well-known political ineptitude comes from my adhering strictly to the demonstrable. A spectacular billboard has more impact than an argument.

BARCALA. The real visionaries were those in Spain and abroad who believed in the rebellion's instantaneous triumph.

MARÓN. Among military men this belief came from distorted professional pride. They imagined that the Republic's life depended on their benevolent silence. Once the army began talking in cannon fire, who could oppose it? The soldiers themselves and those who exploited them did not understand the country's real situation. The rebellion's collapse in Madrid and the zone directly influenced by the capital did not happen by accident; we also triumphed in Catalonia, along the eastern coast as far as Málaga and in the North. Except for some persons' mistakes it would also have collapsed in Zaragoza and Oviedo. If that had happened, the rebels would have been lost with or without the Moors.

PASTRANA. We gain nothing by arguing about that.

MARÓN. In any case, one fact remains incontestable. If votes couldn't destroy the Repubic, neither could the arms of its Spanish enemies, though they included almost all of the

[62]

army, Civil Guard, navy, and more. The Republic had taken deeper root than it seemed.

RIVERA.   Those foreign powers who are now maintaining the rebellion at the expense of all Spain also believed in an easy triumph.

MORALES.   Not necessarily. One can only speculate about it. Note that the insurrectionists sought foreign military aid beforehand merely as a reserve or guarantee for their enterprise, and that Italy and Germany willingly granted it. For them this came gratuitously, an unexpected card in their European game. Clearly both partners recognized the possibility of assistance being needed, but the anticipated quantity remains another question. It may have surprised everyone that the auxiliary forces have turned into the main force, that a sorry rebellion guaranteed by foreigners has turned into a war of conquest controlled by the guarantors. Where Spanish rebels misjudged the state of the country and strength of the Republic's resistance, the foreign despots misjudged all of this and also the insurrectionists' strength. Apparently the Italian government had better information about contingent British policy toward Spain than about the actual situation in Spain. Thus the Italians have played with less risk in London than in the Peninsula.

Italy and Germany lacked good translators of Spanish affairs. Yes! I mean good translators. Spanish phenomena don't translate easily into a foreign language, and for that reason they cannot be understood through a literal translation of terms. Equivalent words don't mean the same thing. Translated into the language of any of the great nations, certain words give the foreigner a false idea of their Spanish meaning, for example: regiment [regimiento], university [universidad], bishop [obispo], squadron [escuadra], Catholicism [catolicismo], Masonry [masonería], machine gun [ametralladora], general [general], school [escuela], agrarian reform [reforma agraria]. It wouldn't surprise me if the rebels had presented the governments of Italy and Germany with a roster of forces at their disposal (the translation of a list of

[63]

terms). Estimating these forces by comparing what the terms signified in their own armies, the Germans and Italians concluded, "No one can resist that," and they committed themselves to a bad or risky deal. Serious resistance came as a surprise, and flaws appeared in the bargain. Now they must go on to save their stake or in hopes of exceeding their original silent partnership.

On the other hand, events induce me to believe that they would have got involved even knowing the actual cost. Granting an element of risk, testing the blade involved as much danger as wielding it freely. Their highly accurate information about the ends and means of other governments has enabled them to defy the weak ones, like the dog in the manger, and to fill the barn with ineffective protests. However, events have exceeded their hopes. They counted on their rivals' impotence; they have actually had their complicity.

GARCÉS.   That's the point. Consider my list of the Republic's foes, in order of their importance, from greater to lesser: Franco-English policy; Italian-German armed intervention; violence, lack of authority of the republican government; and only last of all the rebel forces. How would July's rebels stand today if the other three elements, especially the first, had not helped them?

BARCALA.   If the Republic should perish and Spain again become a despotism of soldiers and clerics, we should owe it to that farce at Geneva which once seemed to provide a shield for the weak. Ultimately we should owe it to the great democratic nonpowers, not for refusing aid that we would not ask for, but for prohibiting a recognized government, with which they maintained official friendship, from exercising its most basic rights. Infamous! They will pay for it very soon.

GARCÉS.   Don't get carried away by resentment. If these democracies should pay for their mistake in any serious way, it would hurt us even more, now and in the future. It is our weakness that attracts this infamy.

[64]

LLUCH. Your whole concept of infamy comes from the notion that international relations are based on a system of laws and obligations. We remain a long way from that. The infamy of the strong trampling on the rights of the weak compares to that of the big fish that swallows up the little fish. Of course, our struggle is taking place between men who have consciences and the use of reason, not fish. We have had the idea of justice for centuries, and because of this we talk about rights. But it all remains a mirage, a spiritual vision, nothing more.

MARÓN. Men formed the League of Nations to realize international justice.

PASTRANA. Did it ever actually exist? A professor's dream, brought to life by the spirit of wartime alliance. It was never more than an illusion that the states of the world, each of them merely an abstraction based on power and self-interest, could establish a sort of egalitarian republic under the rule of justice. It fluttered briefly in the optimistic climate that spread after war's nightmare dissipated. You know that the optimism didn't last long. In fact the universal league of nations never attained completeness. As regards Europe, when Germany's fleet sank at Scapa Flow, British policy toward the Continent changed. It didn't seem a bad idea to stir up impediments to French preponderance. They returned to a policy of balance, of equilibrium. We will all lose by it; they are now applying their system to Spain. All our wailing about the indifference or unfeigned hostility of the great democracies doesn't come to grips with the actual situation. It seems very unsophisticated to represent relations between nations as determined, or as if they should be determined, by the similarity or dissimilarity of their political regimes. It would be absurd to direct a country's foreign policy in this way. France and England need a friendly government in Spain, allied or subservient. Its political coloration remains a secondary consideration. Further, in both countries many democrats believe that while democracy suits them it remains unsuitable for primitive Spain. . . .

[65]

MORALES.   Our conduct sometimes seems to prove it.

PASTRANA.   You might think that democratic nations could reasonably hope for more friendly policies from a democratic Spain. But circumstances control what lies between the probable and the certain. Right now we are seeing the counterproof of that: neither our democracy nor our rights have benefited us in obtaining even official Franco-British good will. Probably in a reversed situation it would seem highly prudent to all of us to behave as they do now. It happened that way in 1914. Maybe we are now paying the price for our neutrality then. The general public believes anything, but we shouldn't fall into the trap of claiming or blaming things on the basis of ideology. In peace and war nations join together for other reasons, and I see nothing wrong with this. No doubt the triumph of Pan-Germanism would have represented a misfortune, but neither the czar nor the mikado could be called a genuine soldier for the liberty and emancipation of mankind. If the Spanish Republic had held out its hand to Fascist Italy, if we had entered into their system by favoring their Mediterranean hegemony at France's expense, a hegemony that could never conceivably come into our own hands, then the *Duce* would have proclaimed the Republic as a Platonic archetype. Absurd? No. The absurdity would lie in our not doing it and then gaining nothing by our gesture.

MORALES.   It would have gone hard with the man who proposed our doing it!

PASTRANA.   That I don't deny. I can see signs of it now in the way people in Spain and abroad judge the aid given us by the USSR. They are making the same error about motivation in foreign policy. The Russians have filled a place in our war that others chose to leave vacant. Naturally, popular feeling, hurt by coolness elsewhere, has rallied to the USSR as our protector. If France and England had recognized our right to buy arms in their markets, the Soviets would have had no military and political role to play ˰re. Then why do they complain? Certain persons, with no proof at all, falsely treat

[66]

the activity of the USSR in our civil war as Communist proselytism. These persons are noteworthy: directors of propaganda in Italy, Germany, and the rebel zone; some upper-class émigrés, fools in all countries, and some people in our own camp. They mislead everyone, but for most it represents an honest mistake; German and Italian propaganda directors have accurate information about the actual situation and deliberately misrepresent it. Other things being equal, the government of the USSR would have sold arms to our republican government even if there hadn't been a single Communist in Spain.

The bourgeois French sign a pact with the USSR contingent on military aid that the Soviet Union could provide them. However, they become frightened when their Communist ally sends us matériel to defend ourselves against those same powers which threaten France, powers against whom their own pact is directed. Forget that fraudulent old refrain about "ideologies." National interests are confronting each other about the security of some, the preponderance of others. If they allow Spain's Republic to perish at the hands of foreigners, England and France (especially France) will lose the next war's first campaign.

MARÓN. They'll find some way to come to an understanding with whomever wins in Spain.

BARCALA. Especially if the rebels win; they have to feel grateful to England.

GARCÉS. Some day learned men will weave a chapter from all of that, no more foul than others in Europe's political history. I recognize its importance; I even recognize that the resolution of our country's drama will depend mainly on decisions made beyond our frontiers. In spite of that, the theme that stirs me up most and the enigma that most confounds me lie elsewhere. My Spanish point of view, quite frankly, concerns itself mainly with what comes after the war. We may win, we may lose. . . . All right. But why has it been necessary that one side or the other win or lose a war? What defect in Spaniards caused them to plunge into this madness?

[67]

Don't talk to me about the politics of the Right or the Left. . . . That isn't enough. What fascinating aberration drives those who are responsible for this crime against the nation?

The foreign invasion ranks as the most obvious scandal. Italian and German armies are conquering the Peninsula to decide the outcome of our civil war for their own benefit. You present this as part of the broader European picture; that also isn't enough. The foreign invasion remains a Spanish event. Let's not forget that. If part of Spain's population hadn't requested and welcomed foreign armies, the invasion would not have occurred. On condition of crushing their compatriots, some Spaniards willingly surrendered the Peninsula to conquerors. Contemporary history shows no parallel example outside of Spain. It recalls interventions during the period of the religious wars, before national feeling and patriotic morale had developed to their present degree. How can we explain this monstrous regression of our country? Or is it regression; have we been mistaken about our progress?

RIVERA. These Spaniards care more about social and religious frontiers than they do about national frontiers.

GARCÉS. Then the nation doesn't exist.

PASTRANA. National patriotism has probably exhausted its cohesive force. Other more compelling impulses are producing new groupings regardless of national boundaries. Patriotism can wait.

MARÓN. Thus speaks the Socialist.

PASTRANA. Socialist and whatever else, I have never stopped being a Spaniard, furiously so since the war. But you'll admit that the Proletarian International may rank as the weakest among these new groups.

MORALES. In our war the Republic, with the support of bourgeoisie and proletarians, espouses the thesis of a national patriotism that pulls together divergent class interests behind a common cause. Conversely, the rebellion, although it calls itself nationalist and exalts Hispanicism, encourages violation

[68]

of our national frontiers as a means of crushing the majority of our population. Somehow, for them, everything that the bourgeois liberals and workers stand for doesn't belong to the nation.

BARCALA.   Only the Devil understands this country.

MORALES.   For more than a hundred years Spanish society has sought a solid footing. We haven't found it yet, and we don't even know how to go about finding it. In the nineteenth century our political confusion showed up in coups d'etat, army pronunciamentos, dictatorships, civil wars, dethrone- ments, and restorations. This present war, as an internal Spanish conflict, represents a grandiose incident in that history. It will not be the last of them. In her short lifetime the Republic hasn't created the forces that are now tearing her apart. For years we somehow ignored enormous elements of Spanish society, even pretending that they didn't exist. The Republic destroyed this fiction and brought them into the light. From the beginning these forces have belabored the government, which has succeeded neither in dominating them nor in attracting their support. Like it or not, the Republic had to develop as a compromise solution to government. I have heard it said that, as a national system, the Republic could not be based on any extremist position. Obviously. But unfortunately no one agreed about the middle course. In their rush to destroy each other the newly exhumed elements of society have upset the balance the Republic offered, and they are pulling her to pieces.

I once wrote that the Republic's backers should make an agreement like that which is attributed to backers of the Restoration. Of course no one paid any attention to me; why should they have? Instead, since 1932 we have seen some republicans conspire with the military, and others (fewer) vent impotent personal ambitions through mindless dema- goguery. But a regime that hopes to endure needs to base its policies on underlying agreements. The unprepared, newborn Republic especially needed this because she owed her very existence to the momentary stupor of her traditional enemies

[69]

and the conditional half-threatening acquiescence of part of the masses. Also she had to evade the extremes of anarchy and dictatorship, both of which flourish in Spain without cultivation. Hence honest tactical agreement represented our only hope; I don't mean pretense or deception. Apparently, however, our climate doesn't suit political prudence. The Republic, lurching, has now come to the point of smashing herself on the rocks of the country's sharp contrasts.

PASTRANA.   I mistrust historical syntheses, especially when they try to prove that we ought not to have lost the battle of Lérida. You're just not well-informed about what has been happening in general or about the importance of certain individual actions in particular circumstances. The reality comes out simpler and perhaps more lamentable.

BARCALA.   Never mind. Let's wipe it all out and begin all over again. They've brought us to this position. Let's take advantage of it to achieve a definitive settlement.

MORALES.   Wipe it all out and begin again! How simple! But why reject all the experience of the past? This is our world; it has got to provide the material from which we will build tomorrow. Only foolish polemic would argue otherwise.

BARCALA.   Thanks. I assure you that war and revolution will finish off those elements of Spanish life which the Republic has not succeeded in dominating.

MORALES.   Are you going to kill off all your enemies?

BARCALA.   I don't want to kill anyone. But revolution and the war in which they have involved us will destroy them.

MARÓN.   After all, the other side preaches by example in their territory.

MORALES.   Thus half of Spain will slaughter the other half?

GARCÉS.   You can't base policy on a decision to exterminate your adversary. It's madness, and in any case impossible. I won't speak of the illicitness of extermination because in times of hysteria no one accepts moral qualifications. However, although thousands of persons may perish, the spirit that motivates them will not perish. Arguably, eliminating everyone who feels a certain way will cause the feeling to disappear, since no one will be left to feel it. But annihilation remains, quite simply, impossible, and undertaking it will spread the ideas you want to eradicate. Compassion for the victims, rage, and revenge all will favor the contagion's spread. In fact, cold-blooded suppression may provoke a sympathetic reaction that is not merely vengeful but ennobling. The whole idea of persecution produces vertigo; it attracts like the abyss. But however tempting the risk, remember that whatever terror achieves, it engenders the forces that will destroy it, and if you try to repress these forces, you multiply their strength.

BARCALA.   One holds power so that one can use it to its fullest against one's enemies.

GARCÉS.   The greatest possible stupidity in exercising power is to use it as though one had an omnipotent hand and an eternal future. Human limits measure all temporal things, and this pertains to power more than to anything else. This conviction operates in the depths of my soul like an invisible bridle; I don't actually feel its presence, but it moderates all of my acts. The enduring influence of my early intellectual and moral training. This sense of proportion substitutes in human terms for Christian ideas of responsibility, or rendering of accounts and expiation. Segismund adopts this kind of morality in *Life Is a Dream;* he accepts prudence in order to avoid waking up in the tower again.

BARCALA.   All of this cool rationalizing, typical of you moderates, doesn't stand up to the test of reality.

GARCÉS.   Rationalizing, reason. Why not? Reason is neither cool nor warm. However, you go to the heart of the matter; only through reason can one recognize what you call reality, think about it, and apply it to behavior. You speak of moderation in a disparaging way, as if it represented nothing but empiricism cautiously clipping the wings of change. That misrepresents it. I have in mind something strictly rational: moderation, sanity, prudence, based on an understanding of actual conditions, on exactitude. I have become convinced

[71]

that Spanish genius is incompatible with exactitude; my observations of our times confirm it. We act like people without reasoning power or judgment. Should we behave like fierce bulls rushing forward into error with our eyes shut? If bulls had the use of reason, bullfights would not take place.

BARCALA. But you will concede that bullfighters and the public do have the use of reason, and they organize the bullfights.

GARCÉS. Because they intend to triumph over one who has no reason.

BARCALA. Sometimes the irrational bull kills the bullfighter. I mean that sanity, reason, exactitude prove useless in the face of tumultuous violence.

GARCÉS. Then we need these qualities more than ever. In a violent storm what will the pilot do? Get drunk or use his skill to save the ship?

BARCALA. Your image doesn't apply; it proves nothing. We are talking about storms in society, not storms at sea. The pilot can't go over to the party of the waves, as if we could even talk in those terms, nor can he judge them. The waves represent a natural force, lacking any purpose. Our present storm is not a momentary, passing, aimless disturbance. It proposes to construct and to destroy; it proclaims programs, good and bad. It uses violence and terror purposefully. You rightly condemn terror, but that's less important than finding out who is right. You may notice that I am working my way around to your point of view.

GARCÉS. No, you're not. Our problem here doesn't lie in finding out which Spanish faction has a better right to govern the country. It arises because some Spaniards use violence and terror to impose their self-proclaimed righteousness and to exterminate as many opponents as possible. And because their victims have also called upon terror in self-defense. It is morally absurd and politically foolish to separate the aim of a cause from the means used to attain it. You don't need terror to accomplish something enduring; it compromises more

[72]

than it helps. And if something is impossible, no amount of terror will bring it to pass. Anything obtained by brute force, or based on it, doesn't last long. As soon as the brutality stops, everything contrived by its evil influence goes out like a straw fire. The rebels have shot thousands of persons in Seville and its province. Foolish men may reckon it up: "So many fewer anarchists." They'll get a terrible shock when they find that the thousands of dead have produced a thousand times more revolutionaries. That observation applies to both sides.

BARCALA.   You stand way above it all and judge the living and the dead like some supreme being.

GARCÉS.   I don't judge. Discuss my arguments if you like, refute them if you can, but don't turn this into a personal attack.

BARCALA.   Actual circumstances refute your arguments. Your thinking achieves nothing. Nobody listens to you. On the other side they hate you for being with us, and we will turn our backs because you don't fully commit yourself.

GARCÉS.   That is the hardship of my destiny. I know it well enough.

BARCALA.   No doubt it flatters your pride to stand apart from others. You prefer self-righteousness, opposing everyone, to sharing the common opinion.

GARCÉS.   No. I look for usefulness in political thought, not aesthetic pleasure. I should like to spread my ideas. Also I doubt that I am alone; many more people than you think share my opinions. If I had the temperament of a man of action I would prove it quickly enough. As I don't, I must satisfy myself with private conversation. In the course of time, when the clamor and havoc have become confused memories, some intelligent person may say that I was right, if by happenstance my opinions survive. By then they will know the outcome of this dispute, and also that we have made a frightful detour to obtain something that lay at arm's length. That we have butchered and destroyed each other stupidly.

[73]

BARCALA. We fight for liberty, for the life and bread of millions of human beings, for justice, for the revolution.

GARCÉS. Let's take that point by point. In the first place, I shall subtract my humble person and yours from the multiple "we fight." Neither of us fights, except with words, and words don't kill. Second, and more important, you confuse the contingent, fleeting present, in which all of this and much more is at stake, with the enduring result of this conflict. Justice, liberty, bread! . . . No doubt about it. But the anguishing thing about this drama without a solution lies in the fact that when it has finished we will have no more justice or freedom or bread than we had before.

BARCALA. Then, logically, when the soldiers revolted we should have submitted to their tyranny.

GARCÉS. I am making allowance for the fact that you don't intend to insult me. Submit? Of course not. We had law, right, order on our side. Everything I have said shows how much I value these words. We had to resist, and to win. This need, this duty constitutes an unavoidable misfortune, comparable even to the monstrous misfortune of the original outrage. The most serious and criminal aspect of the rebellion is that it has created an inextricable tangle with no satisfactory way out and with no possible benefit for the country. I was thinking of this when I said that you should not confuse the present moment with the enduring result. Now, clearly, the future of millions of human beings is at stake. If the rebels win, they will add as many more to the thousands whom they have shot; almost none of us here will escape death. If the government triumphs, horrendous and uncontrollable ravaging by the people will follow. When nothing remains to burn or kill, and a Himalaya of corpses has piled up, if we win, we will not have more freedom, better justice, or more wealth, but a little less and a little worse than before. I won't talk about the results of a rebel triumph! But even they will not enjoy more authority, respect or order than they had before. So grant that I have cause to feel resigned and depressed.

BARCALA. But you forget the revolution. Through it our

[74]

sure victory will avoid the sterility that might otherwise follow from conditions that you describe. The people will make sure that we have a fruitful victory. They aren't fighting merely to defeat the rebels but to carry the revolution forward.

GARCÉS. To avoid antagonizing you, I will forgo any analysis of the content, thought, and acts that you include in the term *revolution*. I will limit myself to reminding you that in calling us to resistance the government called us to defend the Republic, its laws, its legitimacy, etcetera. They included everyone in that call. The conglomeration of deeds that you call the revolution has bred great disorder. Now you and many others proclaim that we must defend all of that. If *revolution* stands as an unofficial watchword, it is a good thing that the government has not adopted it as official dogma. That would create a disastrous situation.

The counterproof makes this clear. Now we can accuse the rebels of having disowned and overridden a legal Republic and can build a case against them on that ground. We could hardly accuse them of lacking respect for the revolution, which no one has established, legalized, or even recognized. So long as we uphold the legal Republic against the rebels, all fault will lie on their side. If we should commit ourselves to upholding a revolution against them, to making them submit to it, then their original guilt would subsist, intensified by the revolutionary clash that they have provoked. However, they would have every right to disown the revolution and refuse to serve it. In seeking peace they will have to surrender themselves to judgment, and legally this judgment should be rendered in the name of the Republic, not that of the revolution. Fortunately the rebels have not quite come to the point of challenging us on grounds of our possibly exceeding legality. Outside of Spain, however, neutral persons do perceive the matter's importance, and when we rightfully invoke our legitimacy, they may ask us about its basis; maybe they are already asking. The problem involves immense danger.

[75]

MARÓN. Social transformation was inevitable in Spain, and within certain limits it was beneficial and just. The Republic wanted to act as arbitrator. This effort and the stupid legend of a Communist threat provided the military rebellion with its pretext and its continuing excuse. The rising has had fatal repercussions. Military indiscipline spurred general indiscipline. Now the river has flooded both banks. The Republic still floats, swept along by the current. To have insisted on sailing against it would have meant certain shipwreck, losing everything, the legal as well as the revolutionary. You must recognize that a revolution exists in fact; I won't deny that it needs control, consolidation. If men have committed outrages and crimes in its name, this always happens with revolutions.

GARCÉS. As a matter of fact, the whole course of revolution is always the same, not only the crimes but all of it, including its outcome. One finds the essence of a revolution in its political content, ideas, authority, capacity to organize, and efficacy in achieving its goals. Under each of these headings the credit of what you call the revolution adds up to zero when it doesn't show a deficit. If you charge the crimes committed against its account, you do your revolution a bad turn because there isn't much else there. Better to recognize the truth and declare that they represent not the revolution's work but latent criminality, motivated by vengeance, greed, hatred, lack of punishment, and plain lust for blood. It is stupid to say that revolution always involves crimes. Even if it always did, though, that would not make them less hateful. I take a more generous attitude than you toward the aborted, mindless revolution. I'm willing to subtract all of that from its account. Perpetual hatred drives Spaniards onward. Not class hatred; hatred plays havoc within each class. Syndicalists shoot each other with a swagger, and rebel bourgeois shoots Popular Front bourgeois by the gross.

The rebels hope to restore the principle of authority based on blind obedience and on suppression of free opinion. Understood in this way, the principle of authority represents bloodthirstiness. Their kind of authority arrogates to itself the power of disposing of the lives of its subjects, and they act as if they measure authority by the number of people they kill. But both sides work wonders in masking hatred as political planning. We posit: all revolutions involve crimes. As crimes abound, we must be experiencing a revolution. Or better yet, through crimes we will have revolution.

BARCALA. Bloodshed repels us all. Your repulsion blinds you, and you don't understand the current revolutionary moment.

GARCÉS. Certainly. No one is less subject than I to the passing moment, revolutionary or not. As much as possible I resist getting caught up. I feel obliged to go beyond these limits, to take a longer view backward and forward. If we don't do this, what do we have? Bewilderment, childishness, bungling, ruin.

MARÓN. In short, if our friend will excuse my interruption, I'll dare to suggest that you stand as an example of political archaism. Nineteenth-century sentimentalism dominates you; it doesn't quite suit our age of iron.

GARCÉS. The rebels ridicule some of us in this same way, as being less modern than they. But the validity of a political judgment doesn't depend on antiquity or novelty. Nothing exceeds the antiquity of getting one's way by blows of a club! However, if I seem archaic to you, don't locate me in the nineteenth century. The roots of my thinking come from the fourth century B.C., twenty-three centuries before you reckoned. You are the ones who stand neck-deep in the nineteenth century, as much in the principal themes of your position as in its picturesque details. The Republic's political and social aims come from that century. It aimed to achieve a bit of the French Revolution, combined with a managed economy and statism. . . .

MARÓN. Spain's political backwardness made that inevitable. The liberal revolution remained incomplete here.

GARCÉS. That's exactly what I'm saying. The International and all of your Marxism, how old are they? A republican statesman has recently and unexpectedly lauded the importance of anarchism in Spain; it dates from the same period. Nationalism, which in modern times inspires our chronic Spanish sense of localism, comes from the French Revolution. The unfortunate slogan that this war represents a struggle against international Fascism seems a distant echo from the legendary "War of Kings" of 1792.

A monstrous understanding of popular sovereignty has made us impotent in organizing a national war effort or national discipline. The president of the Republic spoke recently of demagogic militarism. This has failed to solidify into Caesarism only because we don't have a military commander capable either of obtaining victory or of personifying it. In fact this might offer one way out of our present predicament if things were to go right. If they were to go wrong and we lost the war, we would have communes in Barcelona, in Valencia, and I don't know where else. In other words: we are lost in a very nineteenth-century kind of thicket. Strict calendar limits don't confine the political nineteenth century. It began in 1789 and ended in 1914. It falls our lot to skin its tail. This must come from that political backwardness you talk about.

BARCALA. Speeches! Whether it belongs to the nineteenth or to the twenty-fifth century, Spain is giving birth to a new civilization, a magnificent feat.

GARCÉS. A difficult delivery with no obstetrician. We have more than enough midwives and meddling neighbor women.

BARCALA. You don't believe in the people's creative power.

GARCÉS. 1848! Words, words. The people don't know how to direct artillery fire, or manufacture an airplane or negotiate alliances.

BARCALA. Your logic sounds more anarchistic than the FAI; you are a dissident, a defeatist.

GARCÉS. I will hold my temper so long as you don't call me an Insurgent. If I add up an account and the sum frightens you, does that make it my fault? Can you correct any of my calculations? Surely not.

[78]

BARCALA. Then it all adds up to madness, idiocy, crime. Don't you see anything respectable in our cause?

GARCÉS. Oh, yes! Two things remain respectable; if I dared to use so pompous a word, I would call them sacred. One is the cause of the Republic itself, its right. The other is the self-sacrifice of combatants who face death or sacrifice themselves to it. All the rest remains debatable, depending on one's politics. I allow myself an opinion, like everyone else, and try not to argue about it.

BARCALA. Your opinions have a touch of acerbity, of hostility, that seems unfriendly.

GARCÉS. Then I will keep silent. Our discussion has brought me to confessing point-blank my discouragement about Spain's future. The Republic's ruin and its consequences leave me desolate. Bitterness filtering through may lend my words a misleading flavor. To conclude amicably, I will sum things up with a parable about Spain. Do you want to hear it? Here goes. You know, at least by name, a little village near Madrid, Ciempozuelos. In it there are, or were, two insane asylums. When the rebel attack on Madrid began, Ciempozuelos lay between the two enemy lines; neither side could hold it. It belonged to no one. I don't know whether that remains the case. An acquaintance of mine, bound for its environs, happened to enter Ciempozuelos alone. All of its population had fled. Everyone had left the village except for the insane, who had broken out of their asylum and now did whatever they liked. Only the insane. It seems unnecessary to explain point by point how this exactly represents the Spanish problem.

If you would like to spin out the fantasy, let's see how each side will solve the problem of Ciempozuelos. If the authoritarians, the rebels, enter, they will shoot half of the insane and one more for having said indiscreet things about freedom. The rest they will lock up by main force. If the government troops enter, they will assemble the insane, and a representative of the Popular Front will make a speech to them, urging that they allow themselves to be locked up. They will not agree to it. Then a mixed committee will be named, in which

[79]

the insane will have representation, and as a compromise the committee will agree to lock up 25 percent of them. The others will remain free, and as a guarantee of their freedom the insane will have two seats on the new town council. When the time comes to elect a mayor, everyone will quarrel, and the insane will withdraw in a dignified manner from mixed committee and town council. That is all.

MARÓN. A cruel caricature.

GARCÉS. I won't deny that. Cruel caricatures reveal a lot. Have you ever really looked at one drawn of you?

BARCALA. The weakness in our friend's argument lies in his censuring revolutionary violence on the basis of traditional standards of thought and action, which, in fact, the revolution despises. We can hope that the revolution itself will rehabilitate these standards, appropriate them, and infuse them with new content. Things do happen this way when the revolution triumphs. But until then, from a conventional viewpoint, its progress seems scandalous and ruinous.

RIVERA. From what you've just said, I deduce that the revolution has not yet triumphed. If it has neither aborted nor been conquered, then it must be continuing its ascendant course. In this state a revolution must be fighting something or fighting for something. Does our government direct the revolution?

BARCALA. To a degree.

RIVERA. Is the revolution fighting against the government?

BARCALA. Not openly.

RIVERA. Against whom?

BARCALA. Against the bourgeois class and the capitalist order.

RIVERA. But who represents this class and this order? On whom does the attack focus, or the defense, if the answerable government neither defends those attacked nor is itself attacked directly?

BARCALA. The revolution progresses directly against the institutions, persons, and goods of the bourgeoisie.

[80]

RIVERA.   Of all the bourgeoisie? I see many of them on the side of the revolution and others quite peaceful in their bourgeois way of life.

BARCALA.   Especially against the Fascist bourgeoisie, toward rooting out their economic power.

GARCÉS.   This restriction in a social revolution surprises me. Against the Fascists! You know that it is not that way always, or even most of the time. Let's see how it all adds up. When the government lacks force to put down a military insurrection, a proletarian rising occurs, not directed against the government itself but against the insurrection. The proletarians seize goods and people; many die without a trial. They kill or expel employers, technicians whom they mistrust, and also syndicates, cell groups, libertarian groups, and even whole political parties. They seize real estate, industrial and commercial plants, newspapers, bank accounts, securities, etcetera. We call all of this revolution because it represents something too vast and too serious to dismiss it as rioting.

Now then, a revolution needs to take command, to establish itself in the government, to direct the country according to its views. They haven't done this. Why? Is it lack of strength, of a political plan, of men with authority? A presentiment that even a successful coup would undermine republican resistance, put the rest of the world against us, and lose the war? Or do they abuse their position within powerless coalitions to screen irresponsible plotting, to create de facto conditions that will later sustain them and enable them to dominate the state whenever they choose? There is some truth in all of this.

The revolutionary work began under a government that neither could nor would patronize it. Its excesses came to light under dumbfounded ministerial eyes. The government had the choice of including the revolution's goals among its own goals or suppressing it; inclusion seemed the less impossible. Did the government have sufficient power for suppression?. I'm sure that it did not. But even with sufficient power, using it would have sparked another civil war. A threat of abandoning the front spread, and the government took it seriously. What do you call a situation in which an insurrection begins and does not end, when it violates all the laws and does not establish itself, capped by a government which hates and condemns the revolutionary occurrences and can neither impede nor stop them? You call it indiscipline, anarchy, riot. They could have replaced the old order with another revolutionary order. They did not. Instead impotence and confusion prevailed.

The republican government resigned because the proletarians, even the most moderate, did not support it. It hoped that a government of proletarians, both the parties and the syndicates, which also included some republicans, would have greater authority. But the new governmnt took the same attitude toward the revolution. New ministers who earlier had approved or promoted revolutionary movements now found it necessary to affirm that their primary policy consisted in winning the war, like the former government. They, too, could not adopt the revolution. They, too, remained condemned to enduring it, to temporizing, to trying to control it as if they hoped it would come to an end through discredit or its own exhaustion. The head of the government has said that we have had enough experimentation, indicating his conviction about both loss of credit and weariness. Even the government formed in November with the CNT and anarchists, in difficult circumstances that have not yet been made public, has not successfully annexed the revolution.

For some time the Communists have said that a democratic, parliamentary Republic should remain alive in Spain. I believe in their sincerity because this comes from Stalin. Regionalists and anarchists in the government do neither more nor less than other ministers. Ministers who represent the CNT neither curb nor promote its efforts to take over society, but these efforts continue. For this the presence of their ministers in the government achieves nothing. It doesn't even do much good when they make speeches or write articles against the tactics and more dangerous expedients of the syndicates. If CNT ministers become moderate they fall into discredit, and their former comrades jeer and turn their backs. Reluctant to use its limited means of imposing authority, the government finds itself further weakened by the appearance of a syndical leak, as paralyzing as a synovial leak, at every juncture in public services, including those related to the war. Let's add up the revolution's fruits: disorder, waste of time, of energy and of resources, and a paralytic government. Disastrous for the war effort.

BARCALA.   The revolutionary movement has strengthened our war effort by involving the proletarian class and encouraging its full support.

GARCÉS.   In my judgment subordinate and limited aims that serve the special interests or ambitions of participants in this war are pernicious. The war seeks to repel military dictatorship and tyranny, to preserve liberty for all Spaniards. This should be sufficient to encourage the support of everyone, including the proletarians. If you insist, I can show you that, given the rebels' program, the proletarians have more at stake in our effort than bourgeois liberals. Lesser goals, important for only one group, parasitically weaken the main war effort, since the groups become mainly interested in exploiting any given campaign for their own purposes. If, for instance, revolutionary chieftains think of the war in terms of establishing syndicalism, they won't concentrate their efforts on the military problem of defeating the rebels. If others use the war for future realization of Catalan independence, then they will subordinate their war effort to their nationalist aims.

These secondary objectives rest on a mistaken calculation. If dispersion of forces weakens our resistance and we lose the war, those groups which participated with mental reservations will lose what they have now, what they hoped to gain, and what they had before. This observation is incontestable. Nonetheless, each group concentrates primarily on being the strongest when peace comes so that it can impose itself on the others and on the state. They lose sight of the pressing needs of immediate military problems. To avoid suspicion of treason they advance the postulate of certain victory, and this wipes out all of their guilt. "We will win the war," they say. How? I don't know, since everything that they do destroys their postulate. Another confirmation of the revolution's paralyzing influence on the war.

PASTRANA.   I vote with you. The singular thing about our case lies not in simultaneous revolution and war but, rather, in the continuance in the middle of war of a revolutionary effort that can not, or will not, take over. It persists, frustrating and impeding the government because the government, in turn, has neither assimilated it nor subdued it. The amalgam of war and revolution isn't unusual. A victorious revolutionary movement may provoke a war; war may unleash revolution. Many times a country full of revolutionary fervor has gone ahead to win a war, but always under conditions of effective revolutionary momentum: its authority imposing, its discipline like steel, and acting to unify everyone's efforts through sacrifice, either voluntary or forced. In short, in the face of war, revolution should be like the fasces, an unbreakable bundle of rods; whereas in Spain each of the rods goes its own way. Therefore I believe as you do, that our aborted revolution stands mainly for disorder, and if we lose the war we should blame it on the revolution.

BARCALA.   The government of Catalonia has adopted the revolution, proclaims it, and pretends to direct it.

GARCÉS.   Another rod going its own way, and not one of the lesser rods. Catalonia represents a complex problem, but it doesn't much comfort me. Like the rest of Spain, the government of Catalonia is involved in the war. The government of Catalonia controls its population no better than the government of the Republic controls the population in provinces under its authority. But at the same time the government of Catalonia, because of its ineffectiveness and because of its predilection for secondary goals instead of our mutual war effort, stands as the greatest single hindrance to our military action. The *Generalitat* itself operates in a state of rebellion. While it says privately that Catalan questions have become secondary, that no one now thinks of pushing

[84]

Catalanism to extremes, at the same time the *Generalitat* effects actual separation by assaulting state services and taking over state functions. It legislates where it has no jurisdiction; it administers what belongs to another authority. It uses the FAI as its shield in many of its assaults on the state. Its excuse for confiscating the Bank of Spain: that keeps the FAI from taking over. The *Generalitat* takes over policing of the frontier, customs, direction of the war in Catalonia. For all of this it uses the despicable pretext of preventing syndical abuses; Catalonia complains that the state doesn't help her, then allows her government to fall prisoner to syndicalism.

The government of Catalonia exists in name only. Syndical representatives in this government signify little or nothing; their comrades neither obey them nor fulfill agreements painfully worked out in conference. The decree collectivizing industry was approved as a compromise in exchange for the syndicates' acceptance of decrees for mobilization and militarization. They complied with the first of these decrees but no more. When the *Generalitat* issued fifty-eight decrees at one time, each of them a violation of the law, it couldn't enforce any of them because the syndicates didn't like them. Thus we enjoy the twofold benefit of anarchic disobedience and a *Generalitat* that mixes in where it has no authority.

We can already see repercussions in the war. A rich, populous, hard-working country with industrial power is nil for military purposes. While others fight and die, Catalonia plays politics and has almost no one at the front. It makes one wonder why the rebels haven't tried to break through. If they really wanted to, they would reach Lérida. Although it opposed organization of a useful military force by the government of the Republic, after eight months of war Catalonia hasn't organized such a force. Now, with her citizens calling for an army, Catalonia will discover the advantages of having burned draft records, of having made bonfires of uniforms and harnesses, of allowing the FAI to take over barracks and chase out recruits. Newspapers and men in the *Generalitat* talk continuously about revolution and winning the war. They talk about Catalonia's taking part

[85]

in it, not as a province but as a nation. As a neutral nation, some suggest. They talk of war in Iberia. Iberia? What is that? An ancient country in the Caucasus. . . . If the war is being fought in Iberia, we can relax. At this point, if we win, the state will owe money to Catalonia. Before the war Catalan affairs more than anything else aroused army hostility against the Republic. During the war the plague of anarchism came out of Catalonia. Catalonia has kept an enormous force out of our resistance against the rebels.

LLUCH.   But who controls Catalonia? We must wait and see. The real Catalan people aren't responsible for all of this.

PASTRANA.   The ambitions, divergences, rivalries, conflicts, and indiscipline that obstructed the Popular Front, far from being suspended in wartime, have centupled. Everyone now hopes to gain by direct action that which he could not normally have obtained from the government. The pomegranate has broken into a thousand pieces precisely where divisions were marked, and the case of Catalonia represents another example in this general panorama. Thus so long as the state remains weak, the uprisings and disorders you mentioned will attend the military rebellion. We might have predicted it; we had warnings.

If the rebellion had lasted just eight days, its overthrow would have had strictly political results, guaranteeing the Republic's future. The state would have proceeded with those social reforms which we must achieve eventually. Since the rebellion has turned into a chronic civil war, it has given time and encouragement to the proletarian struggle in all of its forms, the just and reasonable and the senseless and pernicious. We can now see an analogous phenomenon on the local level within the republican camp, propelled by the same social mechanics. The *Generalitat*, insubordinate toward the government, in turn faces insubordination from syndicates that keep it suppressed and obedient. On the fringes I see a reaction shaping up; signs of a revolt against the syndicates are appearing within the forces that stand for public order. They have the support of all peaceful men.

[86]

BARCALA.   In spite of many mistakes, and I make no excuse
for them, this war once again demonstrates that all Spaniards
share common interests. Thus it reinforces our feelings of
national solidarity.

GARCÉS.   Where do you see national solidarity? I don't see it
anywhere. The roof of the house began to burn, and its
tenants, instead of hurrying to help put out the fire, have
turned to plundering each other, carrying away what they
can. This general dissociation has been one of the war's most
miserable aspects, this assault on the state and dispute about
spoils. Class against class, party against party, region against
region, regions against the state. The Spaniards' racial Bed-
ouinism seems stronger than the rebellion itself, so strong
that for many months they have forgotten their fear of the
rebels and concentrated on satiating their repressed greed. An
instinct for egoistic rapacity has come to the surface, an
instinct to grab whatever is handy, whether it has some actual
economic or political value or simply represents pomp and
circumstance. Patrols that break into flats and carry off
furniture are kinsmen to persons who take over businesses or
seize theaters and movie houses, or those who usurp the
state's functions. A rapacious appetite sometimes stimulated
by the irritating insolence of vandals who seem to congratu-
late themselves for their superior cleverness, superior skill, or
some hitherto unrecognized merit. Each has wanted to carry
off the largest piece of the cheese, a cheese that an enemy fox
clenches between his teeth.

When the war began, each province, each city wanted to
fight its own private war. Barcelona wanted to conquer the
Balearics and Aragon, to form greater Catalonia by glorious
conquest, as though operating against foreign territory. The
Basque provinces wanted to conquer Navarre; Oviedo, León.
Málaga and Almería wanted to conquer Granada. Valencia,
Teruel. Cartagena, Córdoba. And so on. Deputies turned up
at the Ministry of War asking for an airplane for their district,
"which is badly neglected," in the same way they had
formerly asked for a post office or a school. And sometimes
they got it! Essentially all of this manifests the foolish

[87]

provincialism, ignorance, and frivolity of the Spanish mind, with some instances of duplicity, greediness, disloyalty, cowardly arrogance in dealing with a weakened state, unscrupulousness, and treason. The *Generalitat* has taken over everything. The improvised Basque government is now playing international politics. In Valencia well-known intriguers and riffraff consorted to beget an infant government. Another sprang up in Aragon, and another in Santander with a minister of foreign affairs and everything.

Well, the same thing happened with the army. No one even listened to the few persons who wanted to rebuild it. Instead each party, each province, each syndicate wanted to have its own army. In the ranks of fighting men, battalions of one group didn't get along with those of another. They played tricks on each other. . . . They rejected the idea of rebuilding a national army on the grounds that it would become "the army of counterrevolution." They were already dividing the bearskin!

Cruel fate: these same persons now scream for an army. Each thought of his own salvation, not the common cause. Political and personal priorities weakened Madrid's defenses by shifting units to Oviedo because presumptuous amateurs said, possibly believed, that otherwise that city would fall in forty-eight hours. In Valencia all the villages armed themselves and posted sentries. They reduced traffic to a crawl and ate paellas, but armed men did not get to the front, which then lay only five hundred kilometers away. They held back to defend their own land. Catalans ravaged Aragon. Petitions came asking the government for their removal. I heard of one of Aragon's self-proclaimed representatives who said that he could not agree to his province's becoming "a trophy of war." A fleet commander's order decided the abandonment of the insane effort to take Mallorca, a move that neither governmental authority nor argument could achieve earlier.

The syndical spirit dominates factories, including munitions factories. Prieto has made it public that when there were no pursuit planes in Madrid, workers at the repair shop in Los Alcázares refused to lengthen their work day or to work

[88]

on Sundays. Since the air raids, workers in Cartagena leave their jobs and the city early so as to avoid danger. After the cannon bombardment of Elizalde in Guipúzcoa, no one in Barcelona wanted to work at night. When the government left Madrid, Valencia came close to welcoming it with cannon fire. Her citizens feared that its presence might attract air raids. Until then Valencians hadn't felt the war. They received refugees grudgingly because they ate up provisions. They feel no debt to Madrid. In short, we have not achieved unity on the basis of a struggle for our common interests.

MARÓN.   You all seem to have reached a state of serious prostration, almost comatose. Do you expect to win the war and govern the Republic without believing in victory or in the Republic's future? Since you are all secularists I cannot counsel a retreat in a monastery; besides, they don't exist any longer. Withdraw, then, and weep for your lack of faith. You probably base your analyses on solid information; we are probably doing as badly as you say. In spite of everything, we will win the war. Spain will provide the world with an example and a model.

RIVERA.   What do you base this on, apart from your faith?

MARÓN.   Since you don't believe in Providence, I'll say on the logic of history. Yes. . . . We do everything badly: war, politics, propaganda. . . . We remain demented and ignorant, barbarians, children. . . . In spite of everything, we will win. How? I don't know. We will win in Madrid; we will win other battles; we will defeat both our Spanish enemies and the foreigners. The League of Nations doesn't help us? Too bad for the League of Nations. Let them bear the shame. France holds back; England throttles us with perfect manners. Well, the day will come when they will turn from their inde-cisiveness and their underhanded bargaining: the day when our legitimacy will shine like the sun because we have overcome foreign invasion. Since the foreign invasion, I believe in our triumph more than ever. The logic of history has certain elements of necessity. A whole people cannot remain subjected by force against its will. Impossible. Be-

[89]

sides, dealing with Spain you must always rely on the extraordinary, the unexpected, the surprising.

RIVERA. Or on the illogical. You provide us with sufficient proof of that.

MARÓN. No. Illogical only if we keep to superficial data and ignore fundamental issues. Spaniards are growing. An effort was made to check their growth by imposing a harness that restrained them, but they shot forward and broke that harness. They will come out of the present crisis full-grown and mature. It lies in the logical course of our history.

RIVERA. Are you suggesting that we should think of the army's rebellion as providential?

MARÓN. Why not?

RIVERA. They say that the ways of Providence are obscure. Let's agree that in this present matter they leave us in complete darkness. If Providence wanted to favor us, it might have found a less expensive, less hazardous way to bring the Spanish people to full maturity.

MARÓN. Don't suppose that I'm suggesting that some supernatural finger pushes or deflects men's actions. For me the providential represents a less crude, less childish concept. I'm not asserting that a provident Deity has stirred up this rebellion. I only say that the free actions of men afford an opportunity for satisfying a feeling of justice, spark of the divine, in our souls. The rebellion is an iniquity, an epidemic of accumulated iniquities. Whatever else occurs in Spain represents justice's vindication.

GARCÉS. Rebels say the same thing, only for them the iniquity is ours and the justice theirs.

MARÓN. It doesn't matter what they say, or what we say either. The event itself transcends our opinions. It holds sway over us all. The inference of your thinking and feeling seems clear: men do not, we do not, measure up to the challenge. I accept this; I deplore it, but it doesn't daunt me. We are not giants. Who could expect that? Could you in fairness reproach anyone for not being a giant? When we win the war,

[90]

perhaps we may come to believe that we have actually transcended our normal limitations. For now, though, let's avoid all that. I can easily console myself for my personal deficiencies, for lack of cleverness, just because our salvation doesn't depend on our abilities.

GARCÉS. I don't think that we should lose anything by having good ministers, good generals, good administrators. . . .

MARÓN. We shouldn't lose anything. But we'll also win without them. You talk as though the rebels were fighting a government whose stability and skill would decide everything, or fighting a regular army whose defeat would mean the war's end. This misconstrues the situation. Not understanding proves our mediocrity. The rebels aren't waging war against our government, against the state, but against the entire people. Governments represent the people; they don't really control them. From the beginning of this war we have only suffered defeats, enough to demoralize and destroy the best professional army. Well, look: we go on very well, but as the rebels take over each additional province, they don't find themselves one step nearer to a final solution.

GARCÉS. I'm afraid that if they continue to take over provinces, they'll take them all, one after the other, and we'll have to defend ourselves on the moon.

MARÓN. They won't take them all.

GARCÉS. That's better. Then we can go arguing. You said that the rebellion's iniquity has initiated a great movement of vindication. For me vindication can only consist in defeating the rebels and punishing the guilty. I accept, I admire the people's rising in the Republic's defense, and I am grateful for it. But you know that monstrous abuses have occurred as part of that rising. The cruelty and vengeance, daughters of fear and cowardice, make me ashamed.

MARÓN. The rebels commit far worse atrocities.

GARCÉS. We know that. No one has a monopoly on cruelty and excess. Moreover, murders committed by the rebels, in monstrous circumstances, have been immensely greater in

[91]

number, and they still commit them. The worst of it, as you said, lies in the fact that these thousands of executions represent part of a political plan. But all of that gives us no excuse. The rebels deny the law; we represent the government, legitimacy, the Republic. Noble behavior with rigorous enforcement of justice would have strengthened the authority of our cause. I was in Madrid that terrible August night when a furious crowd assaulted the prison and murdered some well-known persons. I myself felt like dying that night under their blows. Unfortunately despair did not drive me insane. . . . The president of the Council wept tears of horror. He had reason enough. Did a divine spark of justice start the fire of that massacre? That kind of terror has continued from time to time down to the present; does it form part of the providential plan?

MARÓN.   Don't push me into a corner by rehashing these barbarities. The whole revolution seems alien to me, its good (because much of it is good), its bad, the abominable and the ridiculous. I didn't launch the revolution; I don't encourage it, nor do I profit from its actions. If you want an accounting for its excesses, you should ask for it in the rebel camp. Without the rebellion those persons murdered in that Madrid prison on that day in August, and many more besides, would now remain peacefully in their homes, at their work, in the Cortes, in their courts and offices, in their regiments. They would also be hatching plots against the Republic and calculating the probabilities of a revolt in which all of you would end up murdered. Don't forget the nineteenth of July. If they had taken Madrid (and they failed to take it only because of their—providential—stupidity), they would have shot you, from the president of the Republic to the last doorkeeper in the smallest republican or Socialist club. In those circumstances not one of those who died in August would have moved a finger to save you. After all, they got into this game by their own choice.

People realized this. Anger, cruelty, the insurrection itself did the rest. I'm explaining, not justifying. You and I could not do this kind of thing, advise it, or approve it. But note

[92]

that once rebellion broke out, with its homicidal plans accomplished wherever possible, then vengeance, indignation, and bloody cruelty followed inevitably. It all worked in a pattern of action and reaction from which you cannot remove a single element. You tell me of the murders of Mr. X, Mr. Y, and Mr. Z. I regret them. But they stand as part of the logic of history.

RIVERA.   That too?

MARÓN.   More than anything else. These distinguished victims supported a policy that planted the seeds of the crime two years before, when they killed with impunity in Asturias, tortured prisoners, and lied in both lower and higher courts, including the nation's highest courts. They tried to destroy republicans and Socialists with their slanders, and at the same time plotted to assassinate Mr. X and Mr. Y with police assistance. When after so short an interval I see them fall victims of their own work, I say to myself: logic of history.

GARCÉS.   A meaningless expression. If true, our history must add up to nothing but a flux and reflux of crime. When the other side's turn comes to kill, they also will say: logic of history. I don't accept this system. I defend myself from crime with the law or however I can, but I don't reply with more crime. Had I known the dangerous situation of those people, I would have sheltered them in my own home. I did quietly save more than one person's life, at least from assassination, although they opposed the Republic and had no personal relationship with me—unless they wanted to assassinate me on another occasion.

MARÓN.   You made a mistake.

GARCÉS.   It surprises me to hear you say it, and I can't quite understand how you have come to conform so completely to current attitudes. You, a conservative, who have spent your life upholding maintenance of the law; now you emerge consenting as a matter of course to monstrous violations not just of law but of human compassion and respect for life! What was your old conservatism? Merely a way of getting along in society? Had the values you used to proclaim no

[93]

substance? You and others considered me a terrible revolutionary; did I suffer from delusions in taking the right to life so seriously that I went through anguish about even a well-justified death sentence? What lies behind legality? Nothing? Wasn't it created to satisfy a deep human feeling, a vital and eternal right? You dismiss it with a snap of your fingers and substitute irresponsible violence. It's absurd.

I have seen many people disconcerted by what has happened. Their morality and so-called political thinking have collapsed like a house of cards. I have seen famous "leftists" plunge headfirst into a blind alley, only to emerge saying, "We've made a mistake. This country is not ready for democracy; it must be governed by force." I have seen moderates, who only a year and a half ago were annoyed at being identified as leftist, now declare themselves furious revolutionaries. Men who didn't want to vote for the Statute of Catalonia have converted into anarchistic federalists, flaunting the right of Spanish (or Iberian) people to "self-determination." I've seen many deplorable cases, not counting the fakes. Each has compromised with his fear, his advantage, his ambition.

My own position ranks as most difficult of all. My basic personal ethic has not collapsed. What seemed just or hateful to me before continues to seem just or hateful. I've not put on a mask, nor have I taken one off, because I never wore one. I endure war with a peaceful spirit and the bursts of insanity with my reason intact. Because I refuse all anesthesia, I feel my torment more. I don't want to stop being what I am; I couldn't anyhow. I prefer that others behave in the same way.

MARÓN. It would upset me if you thought of me as a turncoat. I remain conservative; you just don't understand how the term applies to my political temperament. As a conservative I oppose all disorder, not just street rioting but all infractions of the law. Could I align myself with the rebels on grounds that they represent the interests of the privileged classes, the so-called conservatives? Not at all. The rebels and their supporters have given up their right to influence Spanish society through normal peaceful means. They kicked over the

[94]

law in order to replace it with capricious despotism. This represents the greatest possible disorder, the most anarchical. I cannot accept it. I oppose it. Nor does my conservatism mean defense of the privileged. Quite the contrary. To contribute to peace and the conservation of order, I have promulgated ideas of social justice.

Now in the present crisis I support the Republic, not only because it originally represented legitimacy and law, but because almost all of the people stand behind it. With the depletion of ancient sources of law, we must look to the people. The masses can and should shape the basic structure of our future law. Two philosophies of life are contending; a new civilization is taking shape. I affirm the creative power of the people.

MORALES. If our fight is between revolution and rebellion, it appears simply as a struggle between two different ways of dividing up wealth. However, it becomes something less clear and quite different if we think of it as a fight of the Republic, representing liberal democracy tinged with state intervention- ism, against the absolutists of the old Spanish heritage, a struggle between two different philosophies of life. Life means more than the management of property; the character- istic attitude of a people about life depends on racial qualities, on old ferments incorporated into their customs and into their ethical system. The socialization of pastures in a few provinces or control of railroads by a committee of workers instead of a committee of bankers doesn't modify these things.

Build a new civilization? That's a laugh! We haven't completely assimilated the current one, and you see us as building another. I have always feared an involution for Spain, the kind of regression we're experiencing now. Cer- tainly one finds deep veins of civilization in the Spanish soul, even in very backward regions. However corrupted by rural vulgarity, Spaniards still show notable feelings of hospitality, courtesy, and good judgment. We owe this to twenty centuries of Roman culture and Christianity. Language, law, religion have all incorporated us into so-called Western

[95]

civilization. One easily recognizes its lack in the less Christianized, less Romanized districts. But beneath all that, primeval rock persists, unbroken by all the storms. Turning backward always seemed imminent to me, the danger that all of our political and social apparatus would be smashed against that rock. Beyond our great cities the fabric of our civilization remains weak. The ninth century reappears two kilometers from the Castellana's asphalt. Even in the cities one finds significant nucleuses of barbarism, or worse, of anachronistic civilization resistant to all outside influence. This war, in its inception, its purpose, its concomitant phenomena, stands as a gigantic case of regression in spite of its apparently modern slogans. These represent nothing but sterile, pedantic imitations.

Twenty years ago, thinking of the constant backward pull of Spanish society, I amused myself by writing the history of a new Arab invasion of Spain. I told of the great battle of Carabanchel, lost to the sons of Hagar. I didn't think I would hit so close to the mark. In this retracing of centuries I imagined receiving notice of a new Basque revolt against Augustus. Look at them now, fighting not for Spain but for their own laws against Mussolini, who insists on playing Octavian.

Can a people in this condition work out a new civilization, as one might decipher hieroglyphics? According to what you say, we should be bursting with our own strikingly original ideas, the result of a profound intellectual effort or of some kind of new moral crisis. From these ideas, these conditions, we would create a norm valid not only for Spain but for other people of our stock, because your ambitions will extend to Portugal and even to our spiritual descendants overseas. No. Let's not try too much. Forget about civilization. That's too broad a conception, too much over our heads for us to change it through this war of petty generals and committees. The idea that we will invent anything sounds inane to me, like the rebels' proclaimed intention to save Christian civilization in the West.

MARÓN. Then how do you sum up the problem?

[96]

MORALES.   As a problem of freedom, of reason, of human dignity. To introduce a tolerable and tolerant system in a state that is more intelligent, nearer to the social ethics of our times, a state making better use of men's talents and respecting their independence of judgment. Note this last point. I believe that when we've finished this struggle, freedom of opinion will reappear. It doesn't exist now in either of the two Spains. In ours the abandonment seems less forced, but it remains very general, perhaps because of fear. On the other hand, terrific license exists among the administrators who decide orthodoxy. I hope that afterward orthodoxy will disappear. Let them suppress money, property, family. . . .

But let me explain my thoughts. I see many young people, barely literate, precipitantly suppressing other people's beliefs, as though they had discovered warrants unknown to the Holy Office of the Inquisition. They're making a mistake. But if we must suffer this disaster, let's recognize it as part of a backward drift toward brutality. I myself will not endure it. If it persists, I'll leave Spain after the war. We've not rejected the Council of Trent's anathemas to start respecting those of the National Confederation of Labor or some other body of that kind.

MARÓN.   You play down too much the importance of events and their consequences. Apart from the outcome, so violent an upheaval must bear fruit. New energies will come from our miseries. We will see a new horizon.

MORALES.   We will see misery, hunger, decadence.

PASTRANA.   Those of us who are middle-aged feel a special apprehension. We've established our tastes, habits, ambitions. The collapse of everything leaves us all alone in the middle of our journey; we don't know what to do. At the bottom of much of our repugnance throbs frustrated egoism and fear.

MARÓN.   You're not supposed to see an epic at short range, objectively. You should read it in history with its fruits already known, or enjoy it when poetry has transfigured and

[97]

elevated it. The men who besieged Troy must have been the Durruti Column of their day. Nevertheless, apart from the event's actual meaning, its artistic transmutation stands as a cornerstone of European culture. Who knows whether some day the Spanish mind will find inspiration, a national stimulus, in this present upheaval, modern prowess?

Our eight-hundred-year civil war, commonly called the Reconquest, has stood as a great quarry for poetry and politics. It doesn't seem exhausted yet. Witness the presence of the Moors in Spain today, and even more the rebels' justification for Moorish aid and our condemnation of it. Also they are trying again to expel the Jews from Spain, part of a very old program. Historically it should lead next to the expulsion of the Moors who remain in the peninsula, procreating themselves. A new example of that reversion you talked about. Do we stand a chance? Will we be capable of building a poetic and political monument out of the present epic?

RIVERA.   In which we republicans and Socialists run the risk of bearing a legendary disgrace?

PASTRANA.   Ultimately our reputation rests on the outcome. If we lose, our successors, under the influence of propaganda, will certainly rate our conduct as stupid, sordid, and criminal. They will blame the rebellion on us, even say that we, the dregs of Spain and of humanity, started it. If we win, everything that has transpired will stand as a monument of glory, of brilliance, of heroism, not only in popular opinion but in the thought of each of us. Our doubts and sorrows, our terror, and disillusionment will become indistinct memories. Our conduct will appear the perfect course, plotted with intelligence, maintained with valor, everything leading to victory.

GARCÉS.   It will never seem like that to me.

RIVERA.   Why?

GARCÉS.   Whatever the course of events, the Republic's foundering seems quite clear. It succumbed in the last weeks of July when it couldn't end the rebellion in a few days. To

[98]

save itself and us from military tyranny it opened the floodgates, or tolerated their destruction by popular violence. Thus it acknowledged its own impotence. Since then the Republic's inspiring stream has remained deflected or muddied. I now realize that very few drank from it, except frivolously or opportunistically. People still remember to invoke its name, but fewer on each occasion. If no one has yet formally disowned the Republic, only a fool would fail to recognize their lack of support as anticipating its demise. They will disown it in due course.

I don't refer, as some of you probably believe, to the so-called political and social deluge. Religious tolerance forcefully introduced into a country of intolerants brought predictable results. Freedom of conscience and worship have been submerged, on the one hand by the murder of priests and the burning of churches, or their conversion into warehouses. On the other hand we find executions of Masons, Protestants, and atheists. This also pertains to other reforms of the Republic, products of its first burst of activity. I'm not referring to all that.

I'm thinking of a spiritual temperate zone unsuited for all aspirations toward the absolute, where the climate does not agree with mysticism or political fanaticism. I had, myself, settled the Republic in this zone, where reason and experience could foster the growth of wisdom. The Republic didn't require a total commitment from every Spaniard, or even a strong commitment, in order to attain its goals for the nation. On the contrary, it had a mission to end restraints on many aspects of our intellectual and moral life, and to oppose the factions in their efforts to impose new restraints. For six years this conviction has remained part of all my judgments about the Republic's future. Not everyone has understood. I conceived of a Republic that would foster our spiritual life, the single and true principle of civilization. If our Republic didn't exist to advance Spanish civilization, why did we want it? From this idea emerged my second intention: to bring to light, to advance, everything valuable in the intellectual and moral order. Those who believed, honestly or not, that the

[99]

Republic meant anti-Bourbonism, anticlericalism, or anticentralism were fools or scoundrels.

In former times state or church laid claims to the whole of a man's soul. In our day this approach reappears with factions attacking each other under various emblems, though their differences seem more apparent than real. We see demagogic emperors sprouting up now, and emperors who espouse public order, mimicking the ancient world's decadent emperors of broadsword and carnage. We in Spain are experiencing something like that declining ancient world, but shrunken to the personal and geographical dimensions of our country. If rule by the sword comes, Spain will not have an emperor but a legate from foreign emperors.

Whatever might prevail against this, with whatever label, a Republic inspired by the great concept I have described could not. With that Republic destroyed I can have no usefulness to its successor, whatever its form. I now have nothing to do with public life. My problem isn't disillusionment; nothing disillusions me. I know that I belong to another era. Men like me have appeared too soon or too late. Or maybe our uselessness belongs to all times and all places. What Spain requires from now on will smash to smithereens everything that I value; it will go against all of my inclinations and tastes. In spite of my good will, I'd get in the way instead of helping.

Don't just write me off as a fanatic liberal. Among innumerable examples of great political ambition, I recognize only two traditions worthy of respect, those headed by Pericles and Trajan. Behind each of them you can place whomever you like. Between them stand only the charlatans, the bloodthirsty, the insane. . . . We can't repeat the Athenian miracle in the conditions of modern life. On the other hand, to play Trajan it doesn't suffice to buckle on the armor and grasp the sword of this Roman Andalusian. You need to be a great man. . . . I don't see his equal today in the environs of Hispalis [Roman Seville]. If he appeared I would volunteer as his secretary and put his proclamations into this fractured Latin that we call Spanish. Brilliant but untimely imitations of Trajan are normally ridiculous, always pitiful. Charlemagne stands as his most illustrious imitator in modern times. Bonaparte won a hundred battles and brought his country to an unprecedented crash with his madness and his glory. Do you know of anyone in Spain today who has achieved anything that equals even winning the battle of Marengo?

MORALES.   You have a right to be gloomy. But now more than ever we must avoid giving in to low morale. The influence of this inauspicious moment may enable us to reach obvious conclusions and go on to develop a philosophy of renunciation, pessimism, etcetera. Everyone would rightly call this the fruit of adversity. It would not have more or less value on that account. On the other hand the victors will probably feel their hearts warmed by success and loudly proclaim their confidence in life, etcetera. Everyone will recognize this as the fruit of triumph. We would not stand as the first example of illustrious misfortune nor they of triumphant criminality.

Our moral evaluation of the actors' conduct in this drama will soon become blurred, perhaps before the men themselves disappear. History will record the brutish event and its consequences. No one is going to develop a valid theory explaining human activity or politics on the basis of our disillusioned reflections or the victors' confident ones. Victors and vanquished, oppressed and oppressors have always existed. In the end everyone dies and no one cares, or better, no one thinks about past sorrows and happiness. Our present crisis represents nothing but a pulsation of history, but because it has fallen our lot to experience it so violently, it seems to have infinite significance. Don't believe it. We've neither taught nor learned anything new. Nothing old either, or so I believe. One learns nothing. What we think we've learned is ineffectual as a warning or guide to how we should live our lives.

RIVERA.   We've learned some terrible things about our people.

MORALES.   You shouldn't judge the Spanish people rashly. Otherwise you will slander them. It's wrong to criticize the

[101]

morality of an ancient people on the basis of observations made during seven or eight months of war and upheaval. Some might say that these convulsions expose the depths of our national soul. Why its depths?

I should like to know how many and what observations you have listed. Only lamentable deeds? Have you even thought of the praiseworthy deeds, the self-sacrifice, heroism, compassion, aid to the defenseless that show up continually? The total of the combatant armies adds up to some hundreds of thousands. The parties, syndicates, how many there? A million, two million? Let's suppose that these are all active participants, not just members. Of the remaining Spaniards, who else participates in war and revolution because he wants to? Everyone unites in bearing it submissively. Twenty or twenty-one million unarmed Spaniards tolerate and subsidize the armed, who not only slaughter each other but sometimes slaughter the unarmed as well. Haggling about the figures in my hypothesis doesn't alter its significance. Now even more than in normal times a minority represents the whole people. Within this minority the rapacious and the criminal also represent the smaller part. Can you judge the whole country by them? Acts of valor abound on the battlefield. Should we say, then, that Spain is a nation of heroes? No. Then must we accept it as a nation of deranged criminals.?

MARÓN. I don't accept what you are saying. We suffer from an explosion of hatred and cruelty. It pleases more people than those on your list. Some remain aloof from war or revolution because of indifference, fear, or just incapacity; they participate vicariously. At this point not a single Spanish man or woman has failed to sigh, "I wish . . . ," with a thousand threats or desires. To whom do they speak? I don't care how you allot them. The immense majority of the nation looks to the efforts of a few to achieve its objectives, and not always silently. That's a fact. These stay-at-homes are the most cruel of all because they enjoy their evil at a distance, without the risk of committing it, without any need to

[102]

overcome a repugnance or fear that might stop them if they had to perform it themselves.

GARCÉS.   Have you just discovered that! Didn't you believe that the political passions of Spaniards could bring them to the point of waging this war of total extermination against each other?

MARÓN.   Whatever I believed, I can tell that this quality of the Spaniards upsets and grieves you, though you sometimes applaud their worst faults as virtues.

GARCÉS.   I have neither a better nor a worse opinion of my people than of other Europeans. Over twenty centuries we have all done approximately the same things, perpetrating the same errors and crimes, and with great difficulty manifesting some virtues. I lack sufficient charity to love all Spaniards in Christ as my neighbors, as doctrine commands. But Christian doctrine is inadequate here and elsewhere in differentiating between neighbors and foreigners. If I consider the Spaniard in his humanity, apart from Christianity, I see pitiful, universal qualities but nothing exclusively his own. Cruelty, pride, cowardice, ambition, these endowments belong to the species.

Civilization, which does not consist in manufacturing tractors but in cultivating feelings and domesticating fierce impulses, tries to restrain our natural human impulses. The great systems that have debated about the world's moral education have not altered our nature. Their rules come from examples manifested in the lives of a few witnesses; their propagation, enforcement, and continuance come through prestige, coercion, and habit. A new vision of civilization doesn't appear suddenly as a spontaneous outburst. It condenses and becomes clear in the brain of some unusual individual from whom it then descends like rain and light. It penetrates as far as it can. The sea shines on its surface but remains dark and silent at the bottom. Moreover, all civilizing systems have adopted rules and customs that seem repugnant and cruel by the standards of other competing systems or

[103]

those of universal reason. They incorporate these customs because of their own limitations or by way of compromise. Also because of its own special viewpoint and its inability to exceed the data of its own experience, each distrusts universal reason.

Systems contend with each other. Man converts them into instruments of death despite their original noble inspirations. How many provinces have been devastated, how many millions of lives sacrificed about whether the Son emanates from the Father or was created from nothing, about the presence or absence of Our Lord in the Eucharist. Practical inventions from the flint axe to the airplane have increased men's power to harm other men. Well, we have used the more exalted values of moral progress even more for the same purpose. Fortunate man! Only he among the carnivorous animals imagines that he can justify his ferocity in the name of the cause he defends. This reflection applies to everyone. It is very foolish to come out disowning the name of Spaniard because of atrocities committed in a civil war, something barbarous enough in itself. Ought we, then, to deny ourselves as men? Vain words because we have no choice.

RIVERA. Coming down on the train from Toulouse, a Frenchman to whom I talked about Spanish affairs said to me, "You people really are rather savage." The truth of it made me blush.

MORALES. It's our turn now. You might have asked him about the *Jacquerie,* or what the *chauffeurs* did, or the Septembrists during the Revolution. At that point France stood as the most civilized country in the world. Or in more recent times, what did desperate Communists do in Paris, and what did the men of Versailles do to the Communists? If your traveler had been Russian, German, or Italian you might have asked him. . . . Or, better, don't ask them anything. Whether we are called violent and savage by a philosopher, a statesman, or a traveler from Toulouse, we waste our time in replying. Spanish sensibility has never ranked inferior to that of other civilized peoples in any epoch; in fact it has ranked

[104]

notoriously superior to some of the peoples who now lead Western civilization.

Contagion from abroad has caused this monstrous outburst that now tears Spain apart and all of its attendant cruelty. Since the 1914 war, tidal waves of barbarism and violence have submerged Europe. The war itself brought much cruelty. Bleeding a continent, ruining it, hardly seems symptomatic of a refined civilization or of gentle feelings. That they did it all, or tolerated it, in the name of national pride, greatness of the state, for freedom of commerce, or autonomy of peoples didn't make it any better. Once one grants that some aims or ends do justify universal destruction, it becomes difficult to rebut the idea that other ends, other aims may claim the same justifying merit. Why can't religious or social fanaticism vindicate a claim as well as patriotic fanaticism? In 1914 the Spanish people, numbed, defeated, cowed, seemed fed up with tragedies and blood. Remember the opposition to war in Morocco and the popularity of neutrality in the World War? We seemed cured of our irascible temper; even our internal discords rarely turned violent, except in speeches. The popularity of the 1909 revolution in Barcelona came from its being directed against war.

The violence loosed in 1914 has unbalanced Europeans' moral sense. No more rights; no more law. Faith only in direct action, appeal to the machine gun. This plague has infected all peoples; it carries off many. Even those inoculated by warning and by experience have trouble resisting it. Spain has seen prodigious propaganda that points to the triumphant examples of Germany, Italy, Russia, and Austria. Primo de Rivera's dictatorship, a lesson in triumphant illegality and intimidation, did much harm. We have reared a generation that disdains intelligence, neglecting study and work, and instead cultivates physical strength and personal insolence. Men formulate political plans with a view to their shock value. Some people reproach the republicans for not having assassinated the conspiring generals in one night, as the Germans did with dissident Nazis. The generals, for their

[105]

part, intended to do just that to republican leaders. Today's barbarous deeds come after a fifteen-year training period. Now we are reaching the moral level of much of the rest of Europe. We have never been so up-to-date in following fashion.

GARCÉS. Unfortunately we outdo everyone else in the suicidal character of our anger. Other ambitious or semibarbaric peoples direct their fury against the foreigner. Only Spain turns against herself. Perhaps every Spaniard has another Spaniard as his worst enemy. He plucks out his own eye in order to blind his enemy. The rebels' humility in dealing with foreigners shows that we are not xenophobic. Propaganda against Masons and Jews (against the Jews whose blood drowns us!) charges that they lack patriotism—a stupid imitation of foreign barbarity, a crusade against ghosts. It didn't seem serious until they used it as an excuse to load rifles and kill thousands of harmless persons. Will foreign battalions feel more patriotically Spanish, battalions that some Spaniards imagine they have hired to kill other Spaniards? I say "imagine" because the real hirelings are not the foreign armies but the very Spaniards who have brought them over. "We can't do it ourselves," they said. "We have too many Spaniards to kill! Come, help us with the killing." When foreigners bomb, burn, and machine-gun, and our compatriots die by thousands, these hirelings applaud in the name of the fatherland.

For many decades we have played the peasant in his corner in international politics. When someone even mentioned the usefulness of taking some other course, he got no support. An active foreign policy might involve Spain in wars where she had little real interest. The country feared living dangerously. Peace above all. . . . Let other people take up their lances if they liked. The horrors of the European war and the striking advantages of Spanish neutrality consolidated our common conviction. Suddenly this prudence, this peace that we took as patriotic dogma, no longer prevents some Spaniards from loosing on their own people the greatest misfortune they have suffered for centuries. In self-

[106]

destruction we are squandering by hundreds of thousands those lives we saved by renunciation. Our cities, our accumulated wealth, fruits of labor that we intended to preserve by remaining neutral, all are going up in smoke. We have spent twenty years standing guard over a treasure that Philip II would have envied, not wanting to use it to improve our nation. Now we are cleverly managing to turn that treasure into a cinder from the heat of this fever. . . . Strange?

MORALES.   Then you confirm my thesis: Spain is a great country crippled by her people.

RIVERA.   Unless the people have changed their nature, how could it have been a great country?

MORALES.   Not only was it once a great country; it always has been. It is now. The Spaniard creates with one hand what he destroys with the other. And he uses his feet to help. The Spaniard tramples his own work underfoot, monuments that affirm his place in civilization, everything that gives him national being and identification. Our most illustrious provinces have been sown with ruins, most of them our own work. I won't even mention places where the very ruins have disappeared. A saturnine genius. Commonly the Spaniard believes in little or nothing, yet he strives to believe and then aspires to the absolute.

GARCÉS.   We've promised not to make rash judgments about Spain. They will come anyhow. After the war we will suffer the arrows of analysis; it will rain little treatises that investigate our national character. It happened that way after '98. By dint of much reflection they succeeded then in clarifying two serious matters: there is little Aryan blood in Spain, and it doesn't rain much. I give up; let's drop the subject.

MARÓN.   The Spaniards' warlike spirit doesn't seem livelier today than a year ago, nor does their antipathy toward an adventurous foreign policy seem weaker. This monstrous weed of war and destruction has grown in an astonishing way. It seems a kind of mutation. On the rebels' side, foreigners keep the war going. On our side everyone knows

[107]

how much work, how many disasters, it has cost to convince even the combatants that we must take it seriously. I'm distinguishing between enthusiasm for a cause and enthusiasm for war. We accept this war; we bear its burdens, but few of us like it.

Today the war aspires to resolve questions much more profound than those which triggered the army rebellion, questions deriving from the rebellion and its tenacity, and possibly unforeseen by its instigators. An immense thicket has grown up little by little. We have more at stake in the contest, or have come to realize that we have staked more than we thought. In this matter you will find virtually no difference between Loyalists and rebels. We don't need subtle analyses or explanations of the philosophy of history to understand that Spaniards are now risking their most cherished advantages, gains, and possessions. All people want to preserve these things; in similar circumstances other countries would have behaved as we have. Things that are worth a lot cost a lot. What the Spaniards are defending must be worth a lot, since they love it so much.

MORALES. Here begin my doubts, or, frankly, my objections. In the first place, violent love for a thing proves nothing about its real merit, whether in the area of intimate personal preferences or in that of public life and popular movements. You shouldn't try to determine the value of a thing by asking someone who desires it, no matter how heroically he may strive to attain it. Especially if he strives heroically to attain it; because we must recognize judgment as more important here than heroism, however admirable and useful heroism may be. Also, clearly, a certain kind of values, let us call them moral values, have no direct equivalence—are even worthless—in material or concrete terms. We can hardly ask: how much is the Republic worth? How much is monarchy worth? Or put it this way: what sacrifice can we licitly agree to for the Republic or monarchy? We cannot assess these things precisely enough to treat the problem in this way.

Perhaps we might turn the problem over to various

partisans for their valuation, but this changes according to their mood. We need an exact proportion between the object and the sacrifice required to attain it. Our friend resolves this easily with: "Things that are worth a lot cost a lot." He bases his formula for estimating worth on the extremely shaky premise that an object's desirability determines its worth. Of course, even when we do find out this proportion we will only have succeeded in adding to our sorrows (given our personal weakness before destiny). I'm getting ahead of my argument in saying this, but we must face the truth even if we can't follow through on a reasonable course. Thus our terrible predicament.

RIVERA. I begin to see what you are driving at.

MORALES. I'll remove your doubts with a corollary: neither monarchy nor Republic, with as many intermediate zones and territories between them as you like, is worth what they have already cost, not to the republicans or the monarchists but to Spain. In other words (from our republican viewpoint): the Republic cannot achieve sufficient benefits to compensate for existing disasters; nor could the monarchy cause so much affliction, even in another century, that we would not welcome its scourge in order to avoid these disasters. Any sensible person from the rebel camp could adopt my statement, putting monarchy where I put Republic and vice versa. To sum it all up: things that cost a lot are not worth much. We have paid more than the fair price and not in proportional shares: our nation has borne the full burden.

RIVERA. At heart you're not a republican.

MORALES. Possibly. But grant that I have performed as one, impeccably. Under the monarchy (not many years ago), you served the king as a bureaucrat and the Conservative Party as a deputy, while I lived by my independent writing propagating republican doctrines. I have not compromised with monarchism, not even to the extent of that simplistic arrangement, a possible democratization of the dynasty. Nor have I taken the liberty of scorning basic political decorum on grounds of my intellectual superiority, as others have. I

[109]

wanted the Republic as a civilizing instrument for Spain, not as a source of mystical rapture. However, in 1930 or '31 in the incubating days, if her advent had depended on me and on a dreadful civil war, I would have resigned myself to not seeing the Republic in my lifetime.

MARÓN. Thus you smooth the way for bullies. It would only take the threat of a strong gang of troublemakers for you to have us renounce basic justice. A great piece of business for all conspirators, and a curious application of passive resistance to evil.

MORALES. Passive resistance to evil clearly involves encouraging it. We are now actively opposing evil by resisting rebellion and military dictatorship. It is our duty.

MARÓN. Where does your motivation come from? Or, better, on what grounds do you accept this as a duty? By cooperating with the resistance you not only contribute to the war's prolongation but also raise the price, which, according to you, neither monarchy nor Republic is worth.

MORALES. If you hound me too much, I'll stop talking. . . . Better, let me confess something. We speak here quite freely. Having heard some very rudimentary opinions, I'm trying to communicate my own. No one will call them rudimentary. They answer to a distress I cannot overcome. Try to understand. One night in Valencia the newspapers reported that Insurgent airplanes had burned the Prado Museum. I don't remember ever having received so violent a shock or suffering so much. What was it? A feeling of abandonment and loss. I wanted to run away from the news, not to talk about it, not to think about it. In the depths of my horror a protest fought to make itself heard, a lament that I would now formulate in this way: "That's enough. At such a price, no." Luckily the news report proved exaggerated. They had saved the pictures, although planes had fired furiously on the museum. My own emotional disturbance gave me an intense sense of the efficacy of intimidating atrocities. It's called German education.

That day my war morale broke, and it has not recovered. If

[110]

I had been directing the war, I would have proposed something. . . . I don't know . . . call it immunity of the beautiful and historic. "Let's kill each other, if you want, but let's agree to preserve the products of our civilization." Working through my feelings, I came to the conclusion that I expressed before: for Spain neither Republic nor monarchy deserves the price we have already paid. Do you deny it? At least admit the possibility of destruction so enormous as to force serious consideration of my thesis. Then it becomes a matter of more or less, of passing the limit or not. In my judgment we have passed it. In yours we have not. You cannot deny the existence of a limit. When do you think we will have reached it, or gone beyond it?

BARCALA.   Never! The cause of Spain, the people's cause justifies any sacrifice.

LLUCH.   Save the principle and let the nation perish. Do you mean that?

MORALES.   The probable middle solution seems even sadder, with neither of the two extremes succeeding: we will not save the principle, and the nation will not perish; it will live on at death's door.

BARCALA.   I would set fire to Velázquez's paintings myself if I could insure the Republic's triumph.

MORALES.   Then why did you write articles calling the Insurgents barbarians for causing the museum fire? They only did what you would have done for victory.

BARCALA.   Unlike theirs, our cause is just. These comparisons irritate me.

MORALES.   No doubt. I don't compare the two causes; more exactly, I don't equate them. I'm not contrasting their worth, but examining a problem of conduct applicable to combatants in either camp. I don't intend to excuse my own feelings; I want to convince you of the need to appraise the benefits we expect from this war. We must not go beyond this estimate; or we must know when we have exceeded it and why. National interest, in whose name we fight, demands this.

You're not educated men for nothing. You're closing your eyes to my question, refusing to consider it merely because it upsets you, like me when I first heard about the museum fire. You can't escape it. To assure victory, would you accept the deaths of twenty million Spaniards? Surely not. You who could set fire to the Velázquez paintings, would you kill twenty million of your compatriots, or order them killed, if a bloodthirsty god revealed to you that the Republic's triumph depended on it? Surely not.

I don't know whether the rebels are capable of reasoning in this way. Their attitude vaguely suggests that they favor an unparalleled collective execution, but one of their great coryphaei has said that Spain would come straight with the killing of—merely—three hundred thousand people. Another has prohibited the shooting of minors under fifteen years of age. So you see, they admit a limit. If they go beyond their limit, they won't admit it.

Would you agree, if victory required it, that all factories and workshops in Spain should disappear? To the burning of all forests, to fields becoming barren, and to the loss of all our metal tools, to our returning to the Stone Age? Well, in another sphere we would have even more serious destruction, and of course we have already had indications more possible and more probable than my two examples. Would we consent, in order to establish the Republic, or would the rebels consent, in order to establish their monarchy, that Spain · lose not only the Prado Museum but all of her museums, that all of her cathedrals be destroyed, that all of her noble cities be reduced to rubble: Toledo, Burgos, Granada, Salamanca, Santiago . . . and so many others? That there not remain in all of Spain one statue, one palace, one arch, one book, so that the tricolor flag or the other would wave over mountains of ashes? Here our real empire still endures, but vulnerable in each of its creations. Our national spirit reposes and recuperates in their permanence. . . . Must I explain all of this to you?

BARCALA. A monstrous hypothesis. What do you base it on? Reality gives it the lie.

MORALES. It's not very exaggerated. Look at Mérida, Toledo, Madrid. We've made a beginning. The hypothesis merits discussion. The value of a hypothesis, after all, lies in its usefulness for finding an explanation. From the way things are actually happening, it looks as though Spaniards would prefer their country's destruction to the triumph of their enemy brothers. In terms of my argument, it seems that destruction of their spiritual patrimony doesn't matter to them, though it has greater value than all of their political disputes, if only. . . .

PASTRANA. Wait! Who says that we don't care? You're playing games with words. This destruction worries all of us. The man who doesn't feel it personally remains distressed on grounds of cultural prestige. In Madrid, didn't you see the collections in the Liria Palace, after its bombardment by young rebel gentlemen, carefully guarded by Communist workers, all or most of whom lacked any capacity to really appreciate them? Yes, it pains us. But what can we do?

MORALES. Can you accept Spain as a lost civilization, with scholars from some foreign institute coming to search for its vestiges in ash heaps?

PASTRANA. I cannot. That's why I do everything possible to win this war, the only way of holding back destruction. Spanish civilization won't disappear; but these threats to it didn't begin with us.

MORALES. My argument doesn't concern itself about blame. We have always agreed about that. Drop this old refrain; it's beside the point.

PASTRANA. Beside the point! It's primary. If we accepted the question as you pose it, that would ultimately leave us with a great irremediable misfortune and the blame still unassigned. My approach not only saves our part of Spain from a stigma that you or someone else might attach to it, but also preserves our Spanish sensibilities. A point of great importance. The heartrending thing about losing the monuments of our civilization would come not from historical considerations but because these things remain current,

[113]

effective influences on our spirit. Even if facts should correspond exactly to your wild hypothesis, in the midst of our grief we would think it more valuable to preserve our original creative spirit; we would prefer making up losses through new creations rather than undertaking restorations. Like you, I find welcome repose in the noble works of our past. However, if their destruction prevents our admiring them or finding identity in them, new revelations can bring us into communion with their spirit as our admiration did before.

MORALES.   If you insist on declaiming instead of reasoning, I'm defeated.

PASTRANA.   The bruised feelings of an artist. Well, I understand them; I can even share them. But we must look beyond them; the world has more in it than art.

MORALES.   If you don't limit the artist to merely exercising his profession, his special talents can clarify the true hierarchy of values by which we should judge a people's life and aspirations. We achieve this concept of hierarchy by thought, not by political and journalistic ranting.

We can also conceive of a nation divided by conflicting value systems as something distinct from the individuals who compose it. A nation doesn't equal the arithmetic sum of so many nationals. Nor does national spirit represent municipal or local spirit raised to the nth power. Each of us must recognize his identification with our nation as having its own special roots. Thus we do or fail to do things as Spaniards apart from our identification with family, syndicate, party, or religion. In comparing the nation's existence, so conceived, with that of individuals who make it up at a given moment, the difference of duration becomes self-evident. The nation endures, flowing on endlessly. Individuals perish and the nation doesn't change. The fact that men indifferently replace other men shows their insignificance as individuals in the shape and value of the whole. On the other hand, after the universal human characteristics, the first thing that distinguishes or identifies a man is his nationality.

[114]

A nation so conceived, with its own life superior to the lives of its nationals, has its own goals and rights. It suffers from needs and conflicts; it requires powers and a system of morality different from those of its members, even contrary to theirs. On behalf of such goals and that system of morality, I maintain that everything happening in Spain, though advantageous and satisfactory for some (and in equal proportion disastrous and painful for others), remains noxious and fatal to our existence as a nation.

If your patience can bear it, I want to clarify my thoughts further. I adopt the national point of view because no other measures up to our present conflict. One might transcend the national criterion, and some have tried it, but without clear results. In any case, that approach doesn't apply to our dispute. I also recognize that the national criterion is not valid for testing all things and all actions. Through its own egoism, nationalism ignores or oppresses some things. We can't apply it to other things because they lack a common dimension to relate to it. Finally, the national state does not demand blind obedience. You have probably noticed that I remain a liberal.

Also I strongly reject the concept of national spirit as something almost zoological, as well as efforts to discover it in voices of the land and of the dead. This gibberish has had and still has Spanish adherents. I derive aesthetic feelings from the land when it is beautiful or when it will accept the beauty that I lend it. I carefully avoid confusing these feelings with the moral order. The dead don't speak. They have never said anything to anyone. Where are the dead? They have turned into dust. No better than us while they were still alive, they taught us everything then, before attaining the imperious authority of death. We may licitly believe that in the past they had no fewer scoundrels, stupid, wicked, perverse, etcetera than we have today. Our most difficult duty today is not invention of new things but reparation of the errors and atrocities left to us by the dead. In turn, we will leave to our successors a clear program of needed reforms.

With these qualifications and others I've omitted, I uphold my conviction as true: conquering or conquered, with

[115]

Republic or monarchy, even now the nation will come out losing. It is paying a colossal and irredeemable price for its political structure. I say this without rancor or spite. If my words sound less than calm, the cause is bitterness. I trust that you taste the same bitterness.

GARCÉS. Your concept of the nation stands very far from our usual conception of throbbing humanity. It seems more an empty form than an eternal, spiritualized being that transcends other beings. We can't know anything about it without putting back everything that you've removed. You remember the school maxim: only necessity justifies the creation of new entities. Your nation seems to me something not only unnecessary but even useless. What is Spain? Four hundred thousand square kilometers of territory with twenty million living men. Note: living with all the painful and terrible or great and admirable things that the process of living involves. The word *Spain* is an abbreviated expression for that part of humanity included in the term. A being, Spain, doesn't exist apart from the sum of Spaniards. When we talk of national fortune or misfortune, we refer to innumerable beings who suffer it or benefit from it. We used to speak of hunger in Russia, not the hunger of Russia, because an emblematic matron was not dying of hunger, nor the nation itself, but millions of subjects of Czar Nicholas or Czar Stalin. France won the battle of the Marne. Who was France? Some thousands of Frenchmen won it for France, for many millions of their countrymen.

The nation represents a living phenomenon, inseparable from the popular masses, and you should not take *mass* as a term of degradation. Ultimately the nation is a kind of popular disposition. We know it, we name it, we mark it off from other dispositions when certain features prove themselves typical and permanent by reappearing invariably in the course of history. The nation is the masses themselves; everything we call national arises from their conduct. They shape their own destiny and endure it. The famous national spirit to which you appeal in your search for decisive norms

[116]

does not flame up from the combustion of exquisite perfumes; repulsive materials also burn in it.

I also disagree with your idea that the nation has roots in the being of each individual. (Here we are merely expressing our opinions, but, after all, opinions divide and rule the world.) The individual *alone* has no direct connection with the nation. The individual *alone* could be a hermit, a savage, the first cousin to a gorilla. National communion develops not in spite of the other groups that you believe hinder it, but precisely through them: family, profession, party, syndicate . . . why not the syndicate?

You conceive the nation as a provisionally empty form with a still undetermined value, like the algebraic x. But the concept of nation isn't something that hangs around the neck of Spaniards like an empty capsule, token of a disinterested rationality whose authority pulls together all their special interests and resolves their conflicts. I'm not trying to demonstrate the inefficacy of national interest in resolving our conflicts; that doesn't need demonstrating. I'm trying to find the reason for that inefficacy. The problem comes from the blunting of our perception of our national interest. Or because our assessment of the national interest remains irrevocably divided, irrevocably identified with its component parts. We beg the question when we merely invoke national interest. This in turn permits the extreme inference that the Spanish nation was never more than a passing phenomenon and now has ceased to exist.

I accept a force that we call national spirit or national interest according to the aspect it presents. Nobody questions this concept. This force works in two principal ways. It shows up in customs, tastes, in sentimental effusions and selfish calculations, sometimes inadvertently and quite naturally, sometimes purposefully in an attempt to show it or in pedantically pure stylistic forms. You are more interested in the second manifestation, and I'll concentrate on that. This consists in deducing a kind of code of a few simple norms from man's accumulated experiences. The whole nation

[117]

accepts these, agrees with them, and respects them. No one infringes on them without apostatizing from the nation. It would be a good thing if this code existed. But its existence and its force would depend on common, if not unanimous, assent, or at least on such broad and strong acceptance that any dissent would seem useless folly. When it does not exist because an indispensable section of the population is determined to destroy it, then you and I will waste our time in trying to set it up again.

The national spirit loses its normative power to the degree that its counsels or the morals it enforces fail to receive unanimous support. (The state adds compulsion to moral duty.) This is because the essential quality of that norm, deriving from its unique position as superior to the nationals' discordant preferences, lies precisely in producing cohesion and unity. Unity of conduct in regard to certain subjects, nothing more. We know all too well that people invoke the national interest stupidly, foolishly through effusions of inept sentimentalism or, artfully, through words that conceal an interest that, even if legal, remains private. A certain industry claims privileges from the state in the national interest. Exporters of fruit and importers of machinery want Spain's foreign policy changed, in the name of national interest, if their trade doesn't bring in enough money. This doesn't fool any informed person. Confusion arises more easily and more dangerously in another sphere. Political parties invoke national interest which they pretend to express in their doctrines. Some religious groups do the same, not in terms of their doctrine but in recruiting proselytes. Some may err in these pretensions; maybe everyone errs in them, since real national interest has no connection with these disputes, or, possibly, even with their consequences. The whole subject is confused and difficult.

However, most people agree that at certain times, in certain matters, an axiomatic truth can emerge from the tumult, to which everything must yield. Only a few truths can be this powerful. Let us posit, for example, peace. Does peace coincide with national interest; will a people rally in the name of peace? Usually no one will call peace contrary to the general interest. But in all wars both aggressor and attacked always invoke national interest to sustain their cause, and a large part of their nations go along with them. What about internal peace and conservation of the material and spiritual patrimony? This seems even more irrefutable. Nonetheless in Spain we have a nation tearing at its own entrails and each of the three or four governments that exist by fact or by law invoking national interest, again with the support of their followers. This means, and it establishes my thesis, that the nation will not restrain itself and rally round a common goal even for maintenance of internal peace, apparently a signal postulate of the common interest.

Where, then, can we find the mandate of national interest sufficient to obtain everyone's assent? Independence? If not that, nothing remains. Opposing itself to the foreigner is the very act through which a nation affirms its existence. It seems to me that even the most alienated members must join together and take their places in the ranks facing the foreigner. Well, here we have Spain cut through by foreign armies that have come to satisfy special schemes of their respective countries. Not only does our national spirit fail to provide a unanimous repulse, but important Spanish factions even welcome the foreigners and assist them. This is not the first time it has happened, nor the second, nor the third. . . . Look at the past: Spaniards don't put aside their discords when confronting the foreigner; they call on him. When he comes without their calling, they take advantage of his presence. They use him to destroy their Spanish enemy. Thus I am justified in saying, in opposition to our friend, that the normative power of the national spirit remains a utopian dream for Spain. We have neither known how to find one clear axiomatic principle around which to reconstruct a shattered national cohesion, nor do we want to accept such a thing.

RIVERA.   Two irreconcilable factions divide our nation internally.

GARCÉS.   No more and no less. I'm demonstrating it, or,

[119]

better, recalling it. An interior frontier, a sinuous line, separates Spaniards more completely than international frontiers separate the whole nation from foreign people. If by virtue of this separation the flame of our national spirit has become forked, I conclude that at least for now the nation does not exist.

RIVERA.   A frontier traced by hatred.

MORALES.   Undeniable. But why do they hate each other to this degree? What have Spaniards done to each other to make them hate one another so much?

RIVERA.   Knifed each other mercilessly.

MORALES.   During wartime. But why do they knife each other? Why do they hate each other to the point of killing?

MARÓN.   Fear begets hatred. One part of Spain fears the other part to the point of terror. Perpetual threat and atrocious retaliation have changed terror into hatred and sharpened our spirit of revenge. This hatred is unjustified. Fear has proved the worst of counselors. It has exaggerated dangers. A traveler writes of the Spaniard's tigerlike energy when he gets irritated. Nothing irritates so much as believing oneself destined for the wolves. But that danger was remote. The well-to-do, or their defenders, had to take the extreme step of revolting to provoke this violent clash between rich and poor.

It was a reckless move even from the rebels' viewpoint. Newspapers might have announced it under the familiar headline "Murder and Suicide." After they had suffered at your hands for a while, revolt struck incipient rebels as serving the national interest. However, in trying to save themselves from a remote danger, they have brought more irreparable harm to themselves than anything they might have suffered. Common sense would have advised them to look to the state to ease their fears, supporting it instead of undermining it. But those who felt threatened identified the Republic as the cause of their fear and focused their hatred on it. Others gave the Republic only conditional loyalty, a poor disguise for contempt. And those who wanted to follow the path of reason, King Sobrino's role in this Field of Agramonte, reacted by raising their hands over their heads.

MORALES. I'm thinking about your corollary: the nation doesn't exist because the national spirit has failed to awaken and unite us behind our genuine common interests. I can't accept this. Contemporary Spanish life seems faster, more violent than in the past, but out traits, our special reactions, our way of life can't have changed. It seems absurd, then, that the national spirit should fail to appear. How does it, in fact, emerge in the present struggle?

You see the national spirit as a force that should bring all Spaniards together behind an unquestionable primary goal, subordinating their individual concerns. You have put together a brief catalog of objectives that might exercise this imperium: peace, conservation of the national patrimony, independence. . . . As none of these has prevailed over our discordant impulses, you see the national spirit defeated in its most characteristic task. The nation, therefore, does not exist. Is that it?

I don't agree. Your research errs from brevity. It arbitrarily restricts itself to a few school themes. Couldn't one think of others? One might suppose that some new, more effectual force has replaced the efficacious motives of an earlier period. We might look to the realm of psychology for manifestation of the national spirit. You said that the worst enemy of every Spaniard is always another Spaniard. That's right. Why? Because normally another Spaniard imposes on us the insupportable burden of tolerating him, of making concessions, or of respecting his thoughts. In general Spain doesn't concern herself with the foreigner. The average Spaniard, not even mentioning those of more humble status, knows full well that ridiculous people, dreadful people, live out there beyond our borders. He rests secure in having nothing to do with them and shrugs his shoulders. Another Spaniard provides the target for his impatience, his anger, and his enmity. Another Spaniard tries his patience, and he seeks revenge. Revenge for what offense? The offense of thinking in a different way. The Spaniard makes his judgments through irreconcilable

[121]

premises. Pedro is short or tall; the wall is black or white; Juan is a criminal or a saint. Spaniards don't want to see that obvious violations of this principle of contradiction can very well extend an argument into infinity or, more agreeably, bring it to resolution in the Valley of Jehoshaphat. Compromises, blurred profiles, gradations of color—these do not represent our style of morality, politics, or aesthetics. Heads or tails, death or life, a tiny grain emerging from the sand. To found an empire in wilderness or desert. Unanswerable violence or cowering renunciation. To live at the same time as a great leader and an anchorite without illusions about leadership. The Spaniard is violent, domineering. Despotic irascibility dozes beneath his carelessness, laziness, disdain.

We are intolerant. I don't know how we compare in this with other peoples. When we burned heretics and witches, all of Europe burned them; only the definition of heresy varied. Now no one does it. Rationalism and moderation of customs brought tolerance. But the European war and its consequences eliminated pity and mercy. Credos contrary to freedom again hold sway. Compared to the Nazi and Fascist credos, the Council of Trent's decrees seem like products of the Abbey of Thélème. Behold all-knowing Germany, fatherland of Goethe. Of course Luther also claimed it as his fatherland, and he represents something more popular, nationalistic, and fanatical; he drove off apparitions of the Devil with inkwells. And illustrious Italy, where has she landed? Everyone is rehabilitating oppression and intolerance, and the surge does not catch us unprepared. This kind of thing lies at the roots of our being. Some shoot schoolteachers; others shoot priests. Some burn churches; others burn Socialist clubs. Descendants of the inquisitors are burning temples. The purifying virtue of fire continues as a Spanish myth.

Moreover, the Spaniard needs to believe in something. He doesn't realize his potential, doesn't "show what he's made of," as the saying goes, until some faith possesses him. Catholic, Moslem, or revolutionary. Then our ardor for domination makes us try to impose our authority on our

[122]

neighbor or to exterminate him, separate him from the national body. You spoke of unity, a dangerous inclination, cousin to intolerance. With us unity is not measured by physical frontiers but by lines of belief. Strictly speaking, our nation has a moral, not a territorial, base. We warm no hearths; we don't love the duration of things. We have a nomadic soul that takes pleasure in lonely wastelands. The Spanish soul carries within itself its own desert, where it dominates.

Spanish intolerance, encouraged by events in the outside world, now blows as destructive as the sirocco. Unification is its political trademark, unification of opinions and beliefs through exterminating dissidents. You spoke of what the rich sponsors of this war have at stake. That I don't deny. But people got stirred up against proclaimed tolerance, not about the great landlords. Freedom of speech and belief don't suffice for many Spaniards; they take offense and feel scandalized, they rise in rebellion if persons who think differently from themselves have that same freedom. For them the nation includes only those who profess the same orthodoxy as themselves. The nation so conceived achieves purification through tremendous amputations. Mere territory seems less important.

We have the spirit of a wandering tribe, of a mystical and chosen people. The cross, with or without a hook; the half moon or some other emblem (also the hammer and sickle) shining in a white-hot sky. Everyone submissive. To go as a pilgrim into the desert and have the pride of saying, I have no enemies within the horizon's reach. So speaks our national spirit in the great event we're living through, and therefore we allow other values normally held as fundamental to perish or to remain endangered.

RIVERA. How about us? We, too, are Spaniards; the national spirit speaks to us in a different way.

MORALES. You make me laugh! We are the antifatherland. Didn't you know that? That's what they call us. It confirms my thesis. On the other hand, we must wait to see how the

[123]

national spirit really does inspire us, or will inspire us. We represent, more or less, the continuation of what Spain has had of independent thought and spiritual freedom. Though brute force has weeded out dissidence, it has not "put straight" all Spanish opinion. Who has not perceived a whispering complaint on the fringes of orthodoxy throughout our intellectual and moral history? We are its heirs.

After a century of superficial, compromised liberalism, we came to believe that the Republic represented the beginning of an era of spiritual independence that respected thought. But not many felt this way. Only a few souls were directly inspired by the grace of intellectual and moral freedom. Education of the multitude along these lines proved a difficult, slow process. In our nation we had to improvise this kind of education, and for some purposes it came almost too late. Neither tolerance nor respect for new opinions characterizes our masses. We must not confuse their ignorant indifference with respect. I fear that even in our own camp this particular norm of the national spirit, which we should have preferred to modify, will cause us some serious embarrassment. It would not surprise me.

We now witness the stupendous spectacle of Spanish people fighting for their freedom. Strictly speaking we are witnessing examples set by some hundreds of thousands of Spaniards on the battlefields, while behind the lines a very large number tremble from fear, or else intrigue to improve their political positions or get rich by buying and selling or otherwise. After the war we will find out whether the combatants now fighting for their freedom understand that they have also fought for everyone's freedom, including that of their present enemies, and whether those in authority behind the lines also understand this. If they don't, a blast of intolerant national spirit will blow from our camp as it currently blows from the other, and we will witness an amputation performed in the name of a unifying spirit with a different symbol. The present Spanish experience will have contributed nothing. On the other hand someone may successfully impress on our compatriots that their sacrifice is

[124]

not limited to the restricted problem of organizing political power. Rather, it represents a magnificent national redemption (many die to save everyone). If we devote ourselves to this ideal, Spain will discover a new spirit and pass, impoverished, saddened, bloodied but glorious through the very zenith of wisdom.

RIVERA. Now I see it. All brothers afterward; forgive and forget. Until the next time!

MORALES. You don't see. Evidently I didn't make myself clear. Political power with all of its consequences will fall to the victor. I'm examining the probability of harmful use of this power and what may happen, given the tyrannizing, secessionist addictions from which we now suffer. In short, the probability that we will not use this great warning as a guide for future Spanish civilization. We have already said that our conflicting preferences and interests trace the frontier of our internal discord. Will we merely solidify that frontier? I fear so because in the course of our history economic motives and ideological motives have already worked toward this result. Will we repeat it all with different names; will we accept the rebels' dialectic?

Let me give you an example. It has never bothered Spaniards to mix with other races. Not only with those who came into our country; in America we have crossbred with Indians and Negroes. Our great Portuguese brothers have done it even more. Well, all right, for centuries during the war against the Moors political and social assimilation didn't take place. More exactly, its prevention represented a determined policy in spite of frequent crossbreeding between faithful and infidel, above all in spite of the fact that the Moslems were just as Spanish as the Christians. Not many Moors came over. If they had, their sojourn in the Peninsula would soon have Hispanicized them. Most of the Moslems here were just Spanish adherents of another faith. Some, of the rural caste, even represented more ancient Spanish blood than the proud Goths who had conquered land and power. Mixing of blood abounded, but as a whole, as a nation, we managed to isolate them, to convince them of their difference,

[125]

to segregate them, and finally to expel them. We expelled them not only from our territory but from our historical consciousness. For centuries our teaching just did not mention medieval Andalusian civilization. A gigantic case of expulsion, originating in overwhelming intolerance that divided the population with internal frontiers.

Our national spirit took shape around a dogmatic principle that rigorously excluded any unorthodox contribution. Right now Germany is imitating the policy of expulsion we followed from the fifteenth to the seventeenth century. The rebels want to do this with us. We represent the antifatherland, another proscribed nation with a vocation for exile or execution. We represent the Moorish ghetto. Once again the Goths have come to Spain in search of power and wealth. If we should lose this war, children would learn for many generations that in 1937 the enemies of Spanish "unity" were annihilated or expelled as in 1492 or 1610.

You'll object: wasn't religion the motive then? No doubt, if we keep to the widespread popular belief, but other, less familiar incentives had a part in it. Some discerning minds recognized them. A Castilian intellectual [of the fourteenth century], also a prince of the ruling family, said something like: we make war on the Moors to recover our ancestors' lands, which they have taken from us, not to impose our faith on them, "because Jesus Christ doesn't want forced service." I can't judge the particular force of various motives. They work together; appetite for expropriation operates under the guise of religion. Actually the Spanish medieval economy depended for both recruitment and enrichment of the ruling class on free acquisition of new land by right of conquest. Today under the banner of the "nationalist" and "Hispanic" faith, wealthy men want to hold on to lands, not to acquire them, to expel peasants occupying them, and to overthrow the Republic, which has taken over and paid for these lands in a very unrevolutionary way. Theologians counseled expulsion of the Moors, the last step in segregation and denationalization; they imposed it on the Crown as a work of moral unification, an act of conscience. Again the economic

[126]

motive acted, but differently from its usual influence in the Reconquest. Now the need lay not in gaining lands but in keeping them productive. Great lords, masters of the land, opposed expulsion because depopulation meant diminished rent. Today when great proprietors retrieve their lands they won't want all workers shot; they will want enough survivors to keep down the price of labor.

Ideas of racial superiority, given the lie by daily experience in the Peninsula, developed indirectly, with all of their social effects, under the guise of religious prestige. The category "Old Christian" provided the basis for nobility, pure Hispanicism, purity of blood. It depended simply and solely on antiquity of religious belief in the family. An obvious difference in America, nonexistent in the Peninsula, brought a more rigorous application of this declarative principle of racial superiority over there.

This has remained the Spanish system of understanding and invigorating nationality; the dissident doesn't belong. Spanish popular movements, those with any meaning, have expressed an opposite feeling. However, for the most part Spanish plebeianism has repulsed this particular injustice only instinctively because very few eminent Spaniards have known how to bring out the pathetic vein of human misery that lies beneath the surface of plebeian coarseness. The greatest have caught it perfectly: Lope in his most brilliant perceptions and certainly Cervantes. Appropriate to our theme, Cervantes has left us the scene where Sancho meets his friend and compatriot Ricote, now expelled from his fatherland for being a Morisco. A refugee in a foreign land, he feels happy because "here they have freedom of conscience. . . ."

Now the rebels are trying to apply to us a concept of nationality arrived at by that method. Their whole orientation encourages rehabilitation of that spirit of exclusion: what they believe that they know and what they don't know, their confessed motives and those which they don't make clear. Their gyrfalcons proclaim them representatives or successors of Philip II's Spain. Imagine how these gentlemen of Philip II conceive themselves, a king who preferred losing seventeen

[127]

provinces in the Netherlands rather than consenting to the propagation of Lutheranism! General Primo de Rivera one day withdrew to a patio in a ruined castle with his henchmen and proclaimed himself a successor of Isabella the Catholic. Why not Almanzor, like himself a victorious Spanish general! A friend of mine demonstrated that Primo de Rivera spoke not whimsically but truthfully; he really did continue Isabella's tradition, but it led nowhere. I fear exactly that for Spain's future if we reconstruct our nationality on the basis of unification through ideological expulsion, in spite of the warning of this conflict.

PASTRANA. Your rhetoric amazes me! Brilliant! You missed your vocation. What a pity that instead of researching use of the subjunctive in the *Crónica Silense,* you didn't dedicate your talents to historical-political-literary polemic with its broader license. What a role you would have played in the Cortes opposing the traditionalists of the Right. By the beard of Karl Marx! What a tremendous battering ram! They couldn't have called you a barbarian or a bonehead as they did me. Besides holding a Spanish doctorate, you have also taught a course at the University of Uppsala and have lectured at Johns Hopkins University. . . . Isn't that so? Very good.

Then, regretting that I didn't have your help in the Cortes, I'll tell you what I think. You all are playing with these concepts: nation, national, nationality. You look at them through a microscope; you peel off their skins, determined to find out what lies beneath and how it works. Wasted energy. You won't find anything useful for our current situation. And because you find that well dry, you come to the foolish conclusion that the Spanish nation has ceased to exist. In fact it doesn't exist for your purposes, as a normative category for the repair of internal divisions in the nation.

Let's agree on the nation as a natural phenomenon. I condemn it as you conceive it, burdened with eternal, self-created moral values. Such a concept of the nation would inevitably represent a conservative, reactionary force. At the present moment that means antirevolutionary. The more

[128]

exalted the universal, human value of something new, the more its individual qualities are lost. Thus any revolution initially plays havoc with what are accepted as characteristic national traits; later investigations sometimes modify that nationalistic indentification. Revolutions never take their direction from the conservative national spirit, though in the long run a nation may draw enrichment from its past, and the revolution may want to appropriate inspiring examples from that past.

MORALES.   Aren't you, as a Spaniard, grieved by what we have irreparably lost?

PASTRANA.   I am grieved. But we get into trouble if we allow that argument to go very far. After all, we don't want to create still another kind of schism. You feel distress because of the damage or loss to the national patrimony. Whose patrimony?

MORALES.   Everyone's. Spain's wealth of assets gives all of us reasons to love her nobly.

PASTRANA.   No doubt. But who uses or profits from these assets?

MORALES.   All of our people.

PASTRANA.   That depends. The expression "everything in Spain belongs to the Spaniards" is no more than a discredited egalitarian theory. We all live from the national productive patrimony, some better, some worse. This patrimony is composed not only of public property but also of innumerable private patrimonies; keep that in mind. You speak as though the national patrimony represented nothing but accumulated wealth and the means of its accumulation. Yet ordinary labor, in various forms, represents a considerable part of that patrimony. Thus, though our property may be very national, we don't share it in common. Think about the significance of that contradiction. Besides our wealth seems to be as little "national" as possible. We call it that only because some hundreds of thousands of Juans and Pedros, its owners, call themselves Spaniards as we do and use the

[129]

national concept as a protection. All of us live from the fruits of our national patrimony, but many live poorly or hardly live at all.

When you talk about national wealth, either in grief about its destruction or in its defense, you must realize that everyone knows that the property being destroyed or defended belongs to Juan or Pedro. Thus its destruction doesn't bother us so much, or alternatively (given the need for everyone's assistance), we try to make this patrimony truly national. This second arrangement seems more logical and more useful because, in fact, it is not a good thing to destroy anyone's property.

The louder the call to save our national patrimony and the more we put this goal before our fundamental military goals, the more determined will be the resistance mounted by conservatives in the name of the nation. Thus your approach risks denationalizing a large part of our population. I am touched by your grief about the destruction of great Spanish monuments. As an unprofitable part of the national patrimony (not subject to money disputes) they more clearly belong to everyone. I share your grief. But you add that your war morale has collapsed as a result. That's serious. I'm going to speak bluntly. Your confession says this to me: you would feel better under military dictatorship with the cathedrals and museums intact than under a triumphant republic with museums and cathedrals destroyed. Because of your culture and sensitivity, you are discovering, perhaps reluctantly, that the difference between your political thought and that of the rebels doesn't seem so great as to justify destruction of many pleasant things. That's your argument, nothing else.

If everyone of your education and class shared your feelings, then only proletarians and those disinherited from this civilization would and should fight the war. With the excuse of protecting these admirable works of art, which our uneducated people can't even understand, you are weakening efforts to extend their appreciation to a larger audience. If we followed through on your premises we would see a rebound of the conservative forces in our society; after all you identify the nation with them. As a Socialist, I hope for more justice in my nation, but not its destruction. We quite naturally mourn our great misfortune, but a great abyss lies between mourning and complete reversal of our position. Pain alone doesn't produce total conversion. We know that some persons harassed by pains of love have become monks; but our conversion to Fascism because of unrequited love for a beloved woman or the burning of some monuments would indicate something else. You have things out of proportion, unless your reaction has brought forth hidden sympathies with the other side. In that case you should join those who have caused your sorrows.

MORALES.   I find unexpected troubles around every corner. I joined in this discussion hoping to get rid of my depression and to gain strength from taking you on. What a failure! Your sarcasm doesn't upset me, but I thought I deserved better. You win. I'm going out to bark at the moon. There is as much smoke in this room as in our heads. Those wiser than ourselves have already left. Good night.

BARCALA.   Poor Morales! You did give him a bad time.

PASTRANA.   People who won't take sides annoy me, that is, the trimmers.

BARCALA.   He hasn't profited from the war.

PASTRANA.   No matter. He's one of those who make a show of their refinement and superiority, who feel themselves too fine-drawn to risk mixing in practical affairs like the rest of us, lest they run into something vulgar. He no doubt dreamed of a Republic of well-bred people, no crowds, a Republic suitable for the Academy of Moral and Political Sciences. We have many such academic republicans. . . . They speak softly, sip cups of tea . . . the English way . . . like a very polite game of cards. But they didn't like being called fools or rascals, taking knocks when the time came to defend the Republic. They've helped to reestablish politics as a game for idle young gentlemen, though Morales himself is not that kind of person.

RIVERA.   Water over the dam. . . . His horror about the destruction of Spain seems noble. You share it.

[131]

PASTRANA. Certainly, but with a difference. It just doesn't occur to me to evaluate monarchy, Socialism, or the Republic in terms of what sacrifice they might be worth. The question, foolish in itself, shows considerable naiveté. Everyone believes that the fundamental conditions of his life are at stake; many are staking their very lives. They have good reason, and everyone has done what he could to make this belief a fact, to push the stake as high as possible. What else could they do? Nor does it interest me to make a general inquiry into the question of whether we ought to settle political disputes by arms. Sometimes a civil war can cut an impossible knot. Let's admit that. But sometimes it doesn't cut the knot and tightens it instead. It seems to me that this is the way things are developing in Spain, and on this basis I can project the last dismal scene of our tragedy.

RIVERA. Let's have it.

PASTRANA. You've lived through some of the war's ravages. Others you can imagine. This evening you've heard reflections on the enormity of our misfortune. Well. Close your eyes, picture as clearly as you can an exhausted Spain: ruins, misery, hunger. Accentuate the shades of black; join Goya and Valdés Leal, Ezekiel's vision with that of the Apocalypse. Multiply it all by your own personal dread, and when you have reached a result that you cannot bear to contemplate, I will tell you that your conception still lacks the worst feature of this war.

RIVERA. What's that?

PASTRANA. Its uselessness. This war is good for nothing; that is, for nothing good. It resolves nothing. I would be satisfied right now if I knew that its only long-range damage amounted to paying too high a price for a regime. We would at least have acquired something, even if it did cost too much. But things won't turn out that way. When our war has ended, the motives that caused it will remain, and the questions about the nation that we have tried to solve with cannon fire will reappear among the debris and piles of dead men, merely aggravated by our struggle.

[132]

RIVERA.   Then nothing remains but to continue without hope.

PASTRANA.   Given our suffering, what you say sounds logical. But though prolonged and rekindled by hopelessness, the war will have an end. Hatred will burn up its own force. Finally enemies will confront each other as they did in July of 1936, but too exhausted to go on fighting. Then what will happen? A being coming down from Sirius would smile with pity. I predict that a tremendous prophet will arise among us and that he will pronounce heartrending, sarcastic chastisement to the people.

RIVERA.   Your predictions leave nothing. You are the complete defeatist.

PASTRANA.   No. Keep my secret. My predictions will apply as well to our victory as to our defeat. Now to bed; how late it has gotten.

RIVERA.   Everyone has gone outside.

LLUCH.   Come on out Rivera. A night like this proves God's love.

RIVERA.   How beautiful and how calm! Even the sea is silent.

GARCÉS.   It suits me. Our conversation stirred me up, and I probably won't sleep.

MORALES.   What disturbing cares interpose themselves between your eyelids and sleep? inquires the poet.

LLUCH.   I have some very strong sleeping pills.

GARCÉS.   I don't want them. I'm afraid to give in to sleep. I prefer to struggle with my thoughts. It shows a kind of hope. Do you know how I feel?

MORALES.   I know the terror of waking up.

GARCÉS.   Look at those two down on the beach. They don't want to sleep either. For other reasons.

BARCALA.   Laredo and La Vargas. . . . Young love.

MORALES.   Life belongs to them.

[133]

LLUCH. They belong to death as much as we do. If you write the chronicle of this vigil, don't falsify it by finishing off with a trivial symbol.

MORALES. I won't write a chronicle. I'll use what I have heard and pondered tonight as a new chapter in my forthcoming book.

RIVERA. What's the title?

MORALES. *Unexpected Voyage to Codfish Island.* My new chapter will relate how the codfish went to war against the tuna and the peace that they made over the bones.

GARCÉS. Satire?

MORALES. Hardly. I'm transposing many observations into general terms.

GARCÉS. Who are the codfish?

MORALES. Everyone and no one. Ourselves, if you like.

GARCÉS. I'd like to read it.

MORALES. As soon as possible. I'm going in now; I still have a little time for writing.

RIVERA. What are the rest of us going to do?

BARCALA. Sleep. Tomorrow is another day.

GARCÉS. One more.

LLUCH. One less.

(Silence. The sea hardly whispers. Night begins to dissolve into a dull gray, attacked by hazy lights. A streak of brightness traces the horizon's curve. Morning birds. A cock's cry. Walls of the houses suddenly livid, an olive tree left intact by the night, the araucaria's sharp profile. Dawn's great ceremony begins, with ever-changing sounds and colors. Agonizing phantoms afflict the man imprisoned in sleep's cocoon; he moans like a lost soul. From the sky planes dive toward the town like arrows. They are already over it. Explosion. Detonations go off repeatedly, in volleys. Cracking, collapsing, dust, flames. Where does such a creature come from? Another passage. Crash of bombs. Bursts of

[134]

shrapnel. People run, howl, bleed. People burn. Only piles of bricks remain of the inn, emitting black smoke as if they were being baked again. The planes, heading east, shine in the sun's rays, invisible from earth.)

Barcelona, April 1937